PAID
TRAINING

To Lindsey
WITH AN
"E"

ATC!

JOHN CERASANI

PAID
TRAINING

LEARN *THE INDUSTRY*

LEAVE *YOUR JOB*

WIN *ON YOUR OWN*

Outskirts Press, Inc.
Denver, Colorado

This book is dedicated to the clients of
Northwest Comprehensive, Inc.
for demonstrating that the concept of this book works.

Acknowledgements

Thank you to Anastasia and Jacob, my parents, my brother and sister-in-law, my focus group (you know who you are), my friends that listened to me talk about this book for months, Jim and Ian for helping a stranger learn the publishing ropes with nothing to gain in return, and all of those who served as inspiration for many of the real world examples throughout the chapters.

A very special thank you to my original clients that believed in Northwest Comprehensive, Inc.—which is the very foundation of this book—and to my former employer for not giving me the raise I asked for years ago.

Entrepreneurs and Aspiring Entrepreneurs are invited to share thoughts and stay informed at:
www.PAID-TRAINING.com

Once your business flourishes to the point where you are offering employee benefit programs, I'd love to partner with you:
www.NWC-USA.com

Contents

Section 1
Big Picture

This first section is going to get you to where you need to be mentally for reading the rest of this book.

Get ready for a journey that will force you to see the big picture in this game we call our careers.

CHAPTER 1

The Concept

When employees are not killing time doing things like attending internal meetings or external events that serve no purpose, they often sit at a desk working for someone else while daydreaming about starting their own business one day. They conceptualize "the next big thing" and wonder if anyone else has ever thought of it. They fantasize about ways to become a millionaire. They plan out how they could start a particular business and do it better than others that already exist, even though they know nothing about that particular industry other than being a customer in it.

These people look online for opportunities in fields that are foreign to them. They explore business ventures they find fascinating—despite never even having a job in that marketplace. They calculate how long it would take them to save up money for the start-up costs and worry about the lack of income for paying expenses early on. Or they search online ads for existing business opportunities and make similar calculations. It may be doodling on scratch paper during lunch, or it may be working out complex spreadsheets; people everywhere have had the idea cross their minds at least once.

The funny thing is that these people are all looking at it wrong. They want to be a business owner, or at least consider being one, but they then let the thought of the costs and necessary training deter them from pursuing it further. They want to jump into an industry that they know nothing intimately about, and expect to pay someone else to teach them how to run it.

They don't even know what they don't know.

Just because you have been a customer or client for a certain type of product or service doesn't mean you already know the ins and outs of how to run that business. Ever heard anyone pitch you the idea of the restaurant or the bar they want to open? And how awesome of an idea they have for it? It kind of cracks me up when the CPA sitting in a cubicle for the last fifteen years thinks he has an earth-shattering concept that's going to make his bar more successful than others.

The reason so many new businesses fail is because people are jumping into industries they do not know well enough while paying somebody to train them on it.

I have a better idea I want to share with you: How about you start a business in an industry you *do* know very well, and *you* get paid for the training you get on how to be successful? Now that's a more earth-shattering idea than "2 for 1 Drinks on Mondays," don't you think?

If you know what it is you want to do with the company you want to start, first get a job in that industry and use your employment there as paid training for assuring your future company's success. If you do not know what you want to do with your future company but know you want to be a business owner, get a job in an industry that will expose you to many different opportunities. Without knowing it, your employment there will be paid training and the idea for your future business will emerge.

Let me tell you about my paid training and how it worked out for me. I didn't realize it at the time, but I was getting paid for training as the astute employee I was at my white-collar insurance job. I was getting paid handsomely and learning things I wouldn't otherwise have had I just started my own company without working for someone else first.

After five and a half years in the industry at two companies, I learned everything I needed to know to do this without working for someone else. So I started my own company and used the knowledge I gathered from my former employers as my training ground.

Now my own little company is very profitable. I am personally making *a lot* more than what I was making at my old company, and I am competing with and winning regularly against the large, billion-dollar, publicly traded firms, the likes of which I used to work for.

And let me point out, at my old employers, I was a top salesperson and was making a pretty decent amount of money. I basically just gave myself a huge raise for the same job. Also, my success didn't come from being lucky. I am able to better serve my clients than my larger competitors, and my clients recognize that.

To think, had I gotten the big raise years ago like I asked for at my old employer, I would probably have never made the leap and would still be working there. I'd be feeling like I'm making a lot of money because of who I am surrounded by and what my employer was conditioning me to feel like. Instead, I took the same job working for myself and gave myself a raise that I never would have been able to reach working where I was at.

The world needs good employees; this is not a bad thing. It doesn't make sense to "give it a try" as a business owner if you aren't prepared, though. Don't jump into an industry you do not know, and don't do it at all if you are more cut out to be an employee. There are pros and cons on both sides that this book will identify.

A big part of the equation in your decision to start your own business will undoubtedly concern the financial side. There are a lot of people who make *way* more money than I do and there always will be; this goes for you too. There's Jay-Z, Donald Trump, Bill Gates, and Oprah, for instance. I don't expect to be the wealthiest person on the planet. That's not the goal—or a realistic goal, at least. Although earning money should be a big factor, being a business owner is not all about that; it's about having freedom and control of your own fate as well as the ability to make your own decisions in how your clients are treated. It's about self-fulfillment, controlling your own destiny, and earning a good living in the process.

That is how I define "rich"—it's a combination of money, freedom, and control. I make enough money where I can do whatever I want (within reason), I don't answer to anyone, and I love working every single day. I'm no longer worried about my next raise or promotion, or if management is going to change the sales rep compensation schedule.

I never had to work for someone else during a down economy, but if you have, you probably also know about the fear of downsizing and massive lay-offs, all of which are things you cannot control. Owning your own company comes with another set of issues/worries; however, I will take those over the other any day!

If I had gone into business before receiving my paid training, there's a very slim chance I'd be where I am today. I wouldn't have had the option of choosing between being a successful business owner and well-paid employee, because I wouldn't have the preparation and skill set necessary for being a successful business owner. I want you to put yourself in a position where you have both options as well.

For five and a half years, I made good money working for someone else, and my learning grew as I paid attention to everything around me. As soon as I stopped growing, I knew it was time to launch my own company and bring a better service to clients. I didn't know it was going to happen and that it was all training until my last six months as an employee. Had I known it was all training from day one, I probably could have left after two or three years.

Whatever amount of time is right for you will depend on

you and your industry. This book will guide you through that evaluation.

What I'm going to share isn't specific just to my industry. This book is going to help you create, evaluate, and implement a model of your own in whatever industry you are in. You will become aware of your situation as you read this book and be able to formulate a plan.

Also, let me be clear on one thing: This book is not a "feel good" book to motivate you to quit your job and start your own business tomorrow. It is a step-by-step process of giving recommendations that will allow you to evaluate if you should be a business owner. If you find it motivating at times, it's because you are grasping some of the concepts and recognizing your capabilities.

Other times, you may find yourself being challenged as many chapters will make you assess just how good you could be as a business owner or how feasible your business idea is. In the end, you will be in a far better position in determining what direction is best for you—owning your own company, or working for someone else.

You have an advantage over me from reading this book as you are now going to be aware of what's going on and have it spelled out for you. Start seeing your job today as paid training.

CHAPTER 2

Get It Right the First Time

"I tried and failed eight times with different start-ups, then my ninth concept hit it big!"

"Who cares if you try something and fail, just keep trying!"

I care. I don't get it and never will. I don't see the point.

How is it a good thing to eat ramen noodles three times a day or lose all your money trying out businesses that may or may not work? Yet, many entrepreneurial book authors and motivational speakers on the subject will often refer to themselves as "serial entrepreneurs" who failed more times than they succeeded but then climax their story with the one idea that hit it big. Great, good for them on the idea that finally worked. I have no idea why these people encourage their readers or listeners to try and execute ill-advised plans—softening the blow with the idea that failure is okay.

They talk about the "experience" you will receive with failed businesses and that this will help you down the road. Okay, maybe so, but there is a better, more relevant way to go about getting this experience. And it doesn't involve going broke in the interim.

I'd rather formulate my plan, strategize, learn the business, and consider the upside and downside while getting paid well in a nice corporate office, versus wondering how I'm going to make my car payment next month. I will get paid for my training and live comfortably, then I will hit it big. Who cares if I'm making money for someone else in the meantime—it's better than losing all of mine.

There seems to be the mind-set in the "work for yourself, start a company" conversation that is widespread in accepting repeated failure. "It's okay if things don't work out, it's okay if you don't succeed." Forget that!

Leon has the entrepreneurial bug. He is always looking at ways to make money in doing different things. He dropped out of college as he just never envisioned himself as an employee; he didn't see the point in getting the degree. Leon exemplifies the value of paid training versus throwing a bunch of mud at a wall and hoping a piece sticks. There are thousands of Leons out there; learn from Leon and don't go the Leon route.

His first endeavor was buying a pizzeria at the age of twenty-one. He did that for a year and half and then got rid of it. He had no restaurant or food experience prior to owning it.

One of his many next moves was starting a modeling agency. His girlfriend at the time was approached by some agency. There were promises of exposure and marketing, but the models/talents were paying a fee to be part of the agency. Leon thought this company was running the best legal scam on earth. He figured he could do the same thing but make it more of a legitimate service that brings value to clients. Next thing you know, he had office space and a 100 percent commissioned sales team on the street looking for clients. He learned as he went on and, after a while, was pretty well versed in a number of areas in finding his talent opportunities. Ultimately though, the business failed since other than having his girlfriend approached by a similar agency, he had no experience whatsoever in this field.

Another endeavor involved his newfound interest in clothing lines. He thought he could hire someone to make fashionable designs and then outsource its production to another part of the world. He put together a whole product line and approached retailers. He learned as he went—not knowing anything about the business prior to jumping into it. He didn't know what he didn't know about the industry and eventually went out of business.

One of his many other endeavors sounded like a great idea when he spoke about it. He ran it by all of his friends, and they all thought it was a great idea. He started an organic dog food business. Cute, right? (He had a funny, catchy name for the product; the organic craze was in full effect at the time, this business should work!) But wait, what was his experience in the dog food business? Zero. Despite his best efforts, the business failed and he paid his rent the next month by selling his leftover quantities on eBay.

Leon more or less didn't make a dime during his twenties. His credit score was hurt by difficult decisions he had to make during this decade.

He still had the entrepreneurial spirit in him, but he was starting to realize that he couldn't keep just shooting and missing. He was getting too old not to make any money. He eventually took a job working for someone else in a cable contracting business. He learned the ins and outs of the industry and, with his entrepreneurial spirit, eventually quit his job and started his own company doing that line of work.

He knew what he knew and also knew what he didn't know and had to learn. He understood the industry.

Leon's personal income is now in the seven figures, and his own cable contracting company is still in business and growing. This is the Leon you want to be, the first time around.

His credit score is still messed up from the decade of poverty, but now he is in a position where he can pay for big-ticket items with cash anyway.

What was the point of the modeling agency, the pizzeria, the clothing line, and the dog food business? How did that help him? It didn't. His paid training got him to where he is. I'm sure my adversaries would contend that those experiences somehow helped him . . . no they didn't. Paid training was the best path for him; he should have done that from the get-go. So should you.

What if Leon went on to the paid training path from the onset? Here's what would have happened:

- He'd have good credit still.

- He'd be making the money he's making now years sooner.

- He'd be making what he's going to be making in seven or eight years now.

- Instead of deciding between a Maserati and an Aston Martin, he'd be choosing between a yacht and a private jet.

Okay, so maybe I'm a little dramatic. But understand the point. It is not okay to fail. It is not okay to default on your mortgage or car payment as you were "following your dream." Make sure your dream will work, or don't do it. Come up with a new dream until you find one that is profitable and sustainable. There is no glory in being a business failure.

For some reason, there are successful entrepreneurs who think it's okay to encourage you to fail and somehow almost brag about their failures prior to success. What I did with my life was live comfortably all along then just made it better with my company when I started it. The risk was calculated and limited. I knew the industry I dove into, had a plan of attack, and didn't need to learn as I go. I already had the knowledge I needed.

Which position would you rather be in:

1) A person that lived comfortably and made good money while strategizing and preparing for his future

company, then executed the transition to starting the company and succeeded with it.

Or

2) A person that learned over multiple business failures and then succeeded.

Failure is not acceptable. Choose number 1.

Despite what other books might tell you, don't think failure is okay . . . get it right the first time. Get the paid training you need in order to make that happen.

CHAPTER 3

The Epiphany

As an employee in Corporate America, I was often invited to networking events by vendors. These could be golf outings, cocktail receptions, luncheons or whatever. I recall attending such events and mentally justifying them as "work." Management encouraged my peers and me to attend these multiple times a month.

The reality was that the only people to network with at most of these events were never potential clients, but, instead, competitors of mine who were trying to hire me. Although this wasn't the intent of my employers in encouraging me to attend such functions, they didn't seem to realize that this was actually the case. It made absolutely no sense to go to these. As employees, we do things like this to boost our egos and to feel like we are filling our days with work.

As a business owner, I only go to events like this if I foresee one key take away from me attending: *I will learn something that helps me better serve my clients.*

It became obvious to me that there is a better way to serve my clients than as an employee for a large corporation. I didn't get it before, but it suddenly became crystal clear to me. Let me tell you how this process unfolded in my life.

I graduated from Northwestern University and also attended Notre Dame. At both schools, I played football and had the unique opportunity to be around some highly successful and dynamic people. This included classmates that went on to work for some of the best organizations in the world where high intellect is necessary, teammates that had tremendous careers in the NFL, and some legendary football coaches (including Lou Holtz, Urban Meyer, Bob Davie, Gary Barnett, Kevin Wilson, Charlie Strong, and Randy Walker).

I learned a lot from all these people, but my biggest life lesson didn't come until I had an epiphany, and it didn't come until I was about twenty-eight years old. The lesson isn't taught in school. In fact, society is conditioning us for the opposite.

The epiphany was that I'm wasting my time and life working for someone else, and there was no reason to be doing that in the long-term.

Part of the epiphany was also that we all aren't wired the same. I came to realize that there are many people meant to be astute employees forever. People that are much better off working for someone else, and people that could never be as successful on their own. People that prefer working for someone else and coming to work every day while reporting to their superiors. There are people that *need* to work for someone, and I didn't think there was anything wrong with that. I just knew it was not for me. The facts exposed to me during the epiphany allowed me to better calculate what really matters to me and how I was to go about my career decisions.

I suppose it wasn't the kind of realization that happened with a single event; it was the kind where various experiences led me toward a particular direction. One day, like a pile of bricks, it hit me.

I think the biggest reason it hit me is because I was not happy being in my current job. My unhappiness was primarily based on the fact that I felt as if I was making my company a lot of money but I was not getting paid for it proportionately. My output to my employer was greater than what I was taking in. I started looking at other places to work and getting some decent job offers that had considerably better pay than where I was at.

I realized, though, that these offers weren't as good as just doing this on my own and starting my own company. I realized that if I continued to work for others, I will not control my own fate. I had somebody else in control of my future. I realized that moving to another company with a higher-paying job was just buying me time, and in a few years, I'd be unhappy there as well. I needed to do something bigger, something better.

Do you control your personal and financial future right now, or does somebody else?

Do you think you could be a success on your own, or are you better off working for someone else?

For me, this eye-opening process came with a series of events that ultimately led to this epiphany.

I recall the moment when I realized I didn't anymore respect people I thought I respected and I stopped aspiring to be in positions that people I had once admired were in within Corporate America. I suddenly didn't care about being a manager, or being the top salesperson, or whether or not I was going to "make the conference trip" that year, or if I was going to get stock options granted. I realized my destiny was ultimately based on the decisions of others, and I didn't like it. I realized that all these things were just ways for my employers to motivate me to make more money for them—I was a piece of a puzzle to make money for other people, and so were all of my equally oblivious co-workers. These types of incentives, I gathered, didn't do me much good personally, other than putting a few more bucks in my paycheck each month, boosting my ego with nice job titles, and giving me a free vacation. If given the choice, I'd rather make my own money, hire someone to suck up to me, and fly myself to Hawaii.

Does that sound arrogant to you? It shouldn't. This epiphany was the wake-up call for me, and part of the process was coming to terms with some truths that were not easy to swallow at first. As someone else's employee, you need to go through this same realization process. At the end, you may find yourself best suited working for someone still. However, you need to know all the details prior to coming to that conclusion—details that you might initially not want to believe.

I also started to recognize that I need to evaluate who I take advice from and how much credence to put on their advice.

Shoot, if I kept listening to the advice of my superiors and supposedly successful peers, I would be (1) in a job that made me feel good because of my title, (2) at a "secure" job making way less money, yet feeling rich because I am surrounded by other non-rich people, and (3) miserable and hoping some-one else determines my future by giving me a promotion or a raise. Finally, I woke up and stopped taking advice from people with lives that I did not aspire to have.

How much value do you currently put into things like your job title?

Do you find yourself hoping your boss comes through with the raise you believe you earned?

My epiphany led me to analyzing my job in Corporate America, figuring out a way to better serve clients, and then quitting my job and finding clients that would listen.

CHAPTER 4

Employees Are Some of the Smartest People I Know

I'm not the smartest guy on the planet. I was never a valedictorian. I grew up in a middle-class suburb with outstanding parents and an older brother who was a great role model, but not a family filled with business-minded people. The epiphany I had is the only reason I am now doing what I am doing. I want you to have this same epiphany and then make the decision that fits best for you after considerable evaluation.

Many people are smarter than me who make less money and work a lot harder.

A couple of my friends are lawyers at highly reputable national law firms in Chicago. I noticed that there are many nights they had to work until 2:00 a.m. "on a case" their firm was handling. We were out to dinner one night and I asked them if it ever annoys them that business owners with limited formal education can make more money than people in "noble" professions, like lawyers and doctors. They both got a kick out of my question and acknowledged the truth of it.

After a brief chuckle on my comment, they then talked about being a "partner" one day at their firm and how the payoff was going to be huge for them. I then asked who determines if one becomes a partner? They had long explanations of how that worked, but I am able to simplify it for you by saying "not them." They are not fully in control of their career outcome. Not because they are lawyers, but because they work for someone else.

Additionally, they admittedly will be working just as hard, if not harder, when they becomes partners at the firm. So, great, *maybe* they will be making huge money *one day*, but at the price of having to work until two in the morning?

Working long hours and working hard is great, and I encourage everyone to do so, but wouldn't it be better to work those hours for yourself? Wouldn't it be better to have light at the end of the tunnel one day where you aren't working as hard, yet still maintaining your income? This simply doesn't happen when you are an employee.

Some of the smartest people I know are on a path that will never give them the personal and financial freedom they desire. They never had the epiphany I had or went through the evaluation processes that I did. This doesn't make me better than them, but it does put me in a position to make a more informed decision on my life and career outcome. Very few people working for someone else can tell me they made that decision after careful evaluation. However, very few that started businesses can tell me that they went through as thorough of a process as this book identifies prior to starting their own company—which is why so many businesses fail.

At the age of twenty-seven, I was featured in *Chicago Crain's* 40 Under 40 List (an annual list of business movers and shakers in Chicago that are under forty years old). Many of the co-workers at my former company at the time were quick to point me out as a "master of self-promotion," lucky, or somehow not worthy of that accolade as I was, in most people's eyes, a young sales rep that hadn't arrived yet.

I was featured on the list that year because of a company I started in college seven years earlier that had absolutely nothing to do with the line of work I am currently in or was at the time. Nobody at my place of employment was even aware the company existed prior to the issue that I was featured in was published. In fact, the company was well past its prime and barely even running when the list was actually released. It was a social event planning company that I had founded and operated in my spare time. Trust me when I tell you that there were many people in my office that looked a lot smarter than me on paper, yet I was the one on this list—a list that many in Chicago strive (unsuccessfully) to be included in.

I remember co-workers asking why I would be on the list and not my boss . . . because he was an "area executive vice president" and was only thirty-seven years old, and being under forty, he would have qualified to make the list. Here is why he wasn't: His job isn't interesting, and there are a million of him.

Here is why I was: I started a company.

It's pretty simple. In the eyes of most people, working for someone = boring; owning a company = interesting. Whether you think that is fair or not, it is reality. Don't get me wrong, I was a good employee and a top salesperson at the time the list came out. And I did have friends that were happy for me at my company; most told me they thought it was cool—or at least to my face, they did. The editors at *Crain's* picked me over someone like my boss because, well, featuring managers and executives in Corporate America is, quite frankly, not going to sell a lot of magazines.

My boss and my boss's boss were not stupid. I was not smarter or more charismatic than them. They were good at their jobs and in most people's eyes were successful in life. However, they weren't business owners. They were not in that very unique category that puts a person at a whole different level.

I think some of the higher-ups were just a bit surprised or perhaps even a little worried when they saw me on that 40 Under 40 list. Why would they worry? Why would they care? They would care and worry because they had become aware that a profitable piece of their moneymaking puzzle had other options.

The epiphany that I was headed for made me realize that I was, in fact, just a piece of this puzzle. You are part of that same puzzle if you are working for somebody else. It doesn't matter who has the highest IQ in your office. Once you realize that you are just a piece of this puzzle for your employer, you have surpassed your "smarter" co-workers that may never figure that out.

CHAPTER 5

Societal Conditioning

dog·ma·tism
[dawg-muh-tiz-uh m] noun
unfounded positiveness in matters of opinion; arrogant assertion of opinions as truths.

A couple years before the 40 Under 40 List came out, I made a mistake . . . a big one.

Around the age of twenty-five, I had listened too much to people I shouldn't have—people with good intentions in giving me their advice, I might add. I scaled back my event planning company (big time) to focus on my "real" job in the white-collar world. I stopped living a double life and really didn't do much with the events at all anymore. After all, I was a Northwestern graduate and was supposed to be a star in Corporate America; I wasn't supposed to be in a risky, entrepreneurial field, according to the societal conditioning ingrained in me.

I let the advice and comments eventually get the better of me and stopped the company altogether. Not from pressure, but because I actually believed it. I actually believed that being a good, solid employee at a large company was better than being a small business owner—regardless of the industry. I was a piece of a large puzzle, I was brainwashed by society and the culture of my employer to buy into the concept that encouraged people to work for someone else and collect a paycheck rather than work for yourself and have control over your own future.

Do you have opportunities that you have passed up on or opportunities that you have not pursued in order to preserve your current job or career? If so, stop. Learn from my mistakes. Had I focused on my event planning company and not at being a good employee in white-collar America, I would have taken the company to the next level and started doing concerts and other large-scale events. The infrastructure and the popularity was there; I had all the contacts and all the ideas to make it work . . . but I let it all go so I can do what I was supposed to do as a college grad and focus on the job that gave me a 401(k) but didn't allow me to control my own fate in the long run.

You need to have all the facts as you try to determine what career path is best for you. You need to look past what you or the rest of society thinks of as normal, safe, or secure . . . and start looking at the reality. Later sections will guide you in determining if the next move you should make is the same one as mine and *run* from Corporate America, or if you are actually better off staying in it. Either way, there is no right or wrong; the only wrong is if you don't have all the information and if you do not know how to look at it in a way that matters.

When it comes to this kind of decision, most members of our society feel strongly that working for someone else is the best move—often, that's communicated as an arrogant assertion of opinion as truth.

Section 2
The Reality of Working for Someone

This section exposes some of the realities of working for someone else. You may initially disagree with some of them, and you may immediately agree with others. Some readers will not be ready to accept some of the concepts as truths. Everyone's experiences will lead them to different conclusions and different degrees of readiness in understanding the things I am about to discuss.

You may be a top employee and find this offensive, or you may be unemployed and find this obvious. Everyone needs to have this section as a fundamental part of their knowledge base when making career decisions.

Before you dismiss anything you are about to read because it doesn't relate to your industry, because I don't know about your job, because I don't know about your office's culture, or because I just don't know what I am talking about . . . recall the epiphany I described earlier. Remember that some truths are going to be difficult to swallow.

CHAPTER 6

Ego Check—You Are Just an Employee

As you read this chapter, here is some advice:

If you are a successful salesperson, read the words closely and understand them. This does apply to you and you need to understand it . . . especially if you are highly successful.

If you are a support person, try not to laugh out loud if you are reading this at work right now . . . or at least please do not point or look directly at a particular sales rep in your office as you are laughing.

Here are some things that I have heard salespeople say that they think are affirming or positive:

> "I make more than doctors and lawyers, and I'm just in sales."

> "Our top sales guy cleared a million last year."

> "I make more than our company's CFO."

"They are throwing stock options at me left and right."

"They are flying in the president to try and get me to stay."

"I got a headhunter that found me three jobs guaranteeing me 150 percent of what I made last year . . . and last year was huge."

"Our regional VP said I'm next in line for regional manager as soon as one opens up."

My reaction to all of the above: "Who cares! So what?"

Later in this book, I'm going to go through some things that will help you evaluate if you are better off just staying where you are and not leaving to go into business on your own. However, chances are, you *are* better on your own, and I don't care how much money you are making as an employee. An employee is all that you are—just like the custodian in the hallway, or the assistant you have that makes copies for you, your boss, and your boss's boss.

The money you make as an employee could change overnight. Talk to a lawyer and ask him to explain "employed at will" or "at-will employee" to you. It basically means that as long as not discriminatory, an employer can fire someone whenever they want, regardless of offers and comp plans presented in the past. Unless you have a legal employment contract (which most sales reps never have), you aren't guaranteed a thing. Your comp formula that has you making big-time money can change overnight.

And, last but not least, your boss or your boss's boss, who

loves you and has you in the best territory that *you* developed for him, can get fired. You can then watch your territory get split into four parts, because the new boss doesn't want his sales reps making more money than him. Not to mention other areas that can influence all of this, like buyouts and various other market factors in whatever your industry is—none are immune to this.

You don't own the company you work for; that means you are not above getting fired tomorrow when you show up for work. You think you are immune if you are a good employee or are the best salesperson the company has ever seen, but you're not, and you need to wake up immediately. The company will move on without you.

Undoubtedly, some readers are thinking to themselves, "No, not me. John has it all wrong for what I do at my job. This would never happen to me. I wouldn't get fired, I'm too valuable to my company."

Guess again.

Let me use a few real examples that were quite easy to find just from people I know that outline what an "at-will employee" really means. I could have shown a thousand examples; I chose the following three.

Allie worked for a small medical testing supply company. She called on doctors for this company for nine years and developed her territory well. She took the job right after college and was well liked there. She was successful and considered a loyal employee within their organization. She got paid based on 10 percent gross of what she sold; that was her total compensation. One day, her boss told her she was going to get paid 5 percent beginning immediately, and that included accounts she had already sold that she wasn't paid on yet. She went from making about $160,000 a year to making $80,000 a year within a ten-minute conversation. She told me she was going to sue her boss because she had her original offer letter and pay structure in writing. She quickly learned the hard way what "employed at will" means.

Dave was a producing manager for twelve years at an insurance brokerage firm. This was a large organization with thousands of employees. He managed a book of business worth well over $2,000,000 a year to his company in net residual revenue, and he was getting compensated about $230,000 annually. He regularly complained that his compensation was not proportionate with this sized book of business and his management duties. Whoops!

One day, his boss got fired, and . . . guess what? The new boss didn't care about Dave and what he had done for the last twelve years. Ever hear "What have you done for me lately?" Dave eventually got fired, and was replaced with a person making $70,000 to manage the existing book of business. To the new boss, he just saved $160,000 and got rid of what he viewed as a pain-in-the-rear-producing manager that wouldn't stop complaining. Dave learned what "employed at will" means. He was escorted out of the building by security the day he was let go. He was fifty-three years old at the time. He had planned on retiring there.

In my first job out of college, I was a sales rep and had a

regional VP of sales named Steve. Everybody loved Steve; he could walk on water, and I loved him too. He oversaw the entire Midwest and was considered very high up in our company. He sometimes attended our sales meetings when he was in Chicago and always had valuable insight to offer. The company sold health insurance in the United States to employers but was owned by a Canadian company.

Guess what? Although Steve was well loved by all of us, he did not foresee that the Canadians would fire his boss and his boss's boss one day—anyone that was a part of that regime was going to have a hard time surviving.

Steve went from being regional VP of sales to account executive in about seven months. By the way, I was twenty-three years old at the time, and my title was also account executive. Steve learned what "employed at will" means.

Allie, Steve, and Dave all made the same mistake next: They all went to work for someone else, doing the same thing.

Shouldn't they have learned that there is no such thing as job security, especially in sales organizations? Shouldn't they have known they were already in awesome positions with good companies, and the new employer could easily do the same thing to them?

They were all looking for a way to become "employed at will" again. None of the three would have a hard time finding a new job; they are all smart, personable people that most employers would love to have. But why would they choose to again be an "at-will employee"?

Two clichés come to mind when thinking of these three situations. The first is, "Be careful what you wish for." All three sought new jobs as employees, and they got them; they received the compensation and the benefits they hoped for. But they do not ultimately control their future.

The second cliché is, "a blessing in disguise"; unfortunately for all three of them, it was *not* a blessing in disguise, because they didn't look at their jobs as training for themselves. They should have seen the demise of their employment as the time to launch Steve, Dave, or Allie Incorporated. The demotion or firing should have been the wake-up call, the time for the epiphany to hit them, but it wasn't. For most people, the epiphany never hits them—or, at least, is never acted on.

Have you made this realization, or are you too embedded in your career and being a good employee to see it?

All three had the same problem that you will not have after reading this book. They didn't look at what they had been doing for the years prior as "training" to go on their own and start their own company; that was never their goal. They didn't position themselves well for going on their own, and they didn't evaluate every day for the last two, five, six, or fifteen years how they could be better than their employer doing the same thing (or something similar in the industry).

Now all three of them have new jobs and are in decent positions . . . until they go through the same thing again in the future. They are not in control of their fate; their new boss is. They are vulnerable to the same thing happening to them again, just like the CFO, controller, HR director, and administrative assistant are.

Everyone, but the owner, is *just an employee*! This includes *you*!

If you are currently unemployed and looking for a job, reflect upon your past employment experience as paid training. Were you a Dave, Allie, or Steve as an employee? Is it really your best move to seek opportunities to become "employed at will" again?

If you are currently employed and are seeing your employment as "paid training," the chances are huge that you will be the one severing ties with your employer—on your terms.

CHAPTER 7

Lay Off the Company Kool-Aid

I live in Chicago and I'm not a hockey fan, but I can tell you that the Chicago Blackhawks won the Stanley Cup in 2010. I couldn't tell you who won it in 2009 or 2011 though. I can only tell you that the Blackhawks didn't.

It's all perception and relativity.

The woman that won the beauty pageant for Miss Illinois isn't obsessing about who won Miss Kansas. The people that Miss Kansas beat in Kansas are obsessing about her though. Outside of their world, it's just not really that big of a deal.

It's often the employees drinking the company Kool-Aid that make somebody admired or rise to the top of an office. Most times, outside of the organization he or she is in, that person doesn't mean a thing— at least not any more than anyone else in that office.

A friend of mine was a rookie salesperson at a big company, and the sales manager was out with him at a bar after a Cubs game; I was at the game as well. He wanted to introduce this guy to me, so he asked me to meet up with them, and I did.

In private later on, he was asking me how impressed I was and kept going on about how awesome the guy was. The guy wasn't any more impressive than my HVAC repair person. Actually, that isn't fair; my HVAC repair man is a sharp guy that started his own company. He is far more impressive than this person. The person I am referring to didn't have any redeeming qualities that made him admirable, only that he had a bunch of people under him that laughed at all of his jokes and sucked up to him. There was nothing that made him stand out. Employees are common. Business owners are unique.

Employees are not bad people. They can be smart and successful. The world does need good employees. The point of my previous paragraph is that big-title people are put on a pedestal by people in that organization. To everyone else, they aren't important.

Business owners, on the other hand, are always important and looked at as impressive and admirable to people everywhere. There is a reason for that; they had the courage and wherewithal to leave their secure company job and start their own venture.

Employees at big corporations like to pretend they are better than owners of much-smaller competitors, but they often only make a fraction of what they make in income and have little to no control of their future. They don't get it, and they can't get it because they are drinking too much Kool-Aid. They have their co-workers on the same boat to justify their existence.

Their company has ingrained in them the belief that they are better off collecting a paycheck instead of being on their own. They believe it and give each other high fives at happy hour talking office politics while pretending their drinks were with a client so they can sneak it on their expense report. Business owners don't do things like this.

The problem is, the aforementioned rookie-salesperson friend is in an organization surrounded by a bunch of people kissing the rear ends of the same people, and he has adapted to a culture that the company wants the employees to have. That culture will often make top salespeople and sales managers look like God—it doesn't have to be salespeople though. The fact of the matter is that outside of that office, nobody cares. They are just employees like everyone else in the office. They are living in a fantasy world that makes them feel more important or richer because of who they are surrounded by. Look at Allie, Steve, and Dave from the last chapter; all were people who were admired in their offices—and all of them got screwed somehow by their companies . . . here today and gone tomorrow and their boss at their next job isn't going to care about their accolades working for someone else in the past.

As you read the last paragraph, you should have felt one of two things. One would be that you immediately thought of who the "walk on water" person is in your office; the other is, you realized you are or might be that person. Let me tell you, neither is right or wrong. Whether you are the rear end kisser or the rear end kissee in your office, wouldn't it be better to take control of your own destiny?

◄ PAID TRAINING

Outside of your company, nobody cares who the top salesperson is, where the manager got his MBA from, or anything else . . . only you and your co-workers do. STOP DRINKING THE KOOL-AID!

CHAPTER **8**

The Invisible Man

One of the toughest things to swallow as a college football player is how you are treated if you become injured to the point where you are unable to perform or play. It doesn't matter how good you were before the injury, if you are a freshman or a senior or what college you are playing at. You do *not* exist when you are hurt. You sit on the sidelines during practice wearing a red jersey, and you watch. Nobody talks to you, nobody asks you anything; you just sit and watch. It isn't your fault that you got hurt; you didn't do anything wrong. It just happened. Now you don't exist in the coach's eyes. You cannot help the team win this weekend. You are irrelevant. It's just the way it is.

There are many jobs that have external factors that can cripple one's performance. This is especially true in sales. It could be a regional competitor having ridiculous limited-time offers that your company simply cannot compete with. It could be some news in the local media about your company that makes prospective new clients very concerned about partnering with you. It could be any number of things that are simply *not* your fault.

Let's assume that this is limited to just your territory and not companywide. No matter how successful you were in the past, watch how fast your accolades are forgotten. Watch how fast you don't matter. You are a hurt college football player, and if you stay hurt too long, you won't have a job.

In a sales environment, the office's sales goals are the football game. If you aren't doing anything to help get to that, you don't exist. Depending on where you are employed and the particulars of that operation, there may be assistance—kind of like rehabilitating the knee injury so you could play in the game next weekend. But if that knee remains hurt and doesn't fix itself, it really doesn't matter what the reason is; the bottom line is that you cannot help the team win and you are not bringing anything to the table now. You need to get cut from the team because you're taking up space, even though you scored three touchdowns the week before your injury.

Take the case of Greg. Greg worked in IT sales in his first position after graduating from an Ivy League school. Right out of the gates, he found success. He was young and had the energy and motivation that many prospective clients took a liking to. To build his confidence, he went after the smaller deals and was closing them left and right. He gained confidence and slowly built up to larger accounts in his second and third year on the job. He was quickly becoming recognized as the company's future star, and he began getting encouraged by upper management to start going "whale hunting"—going after the jumbo accounts.

The sales cycle was much longer, but Greg tenaciously pursued these and did everything the way he was encouraged to do so by his superiors. However, in the eleventh hour of his first "jumbo" being closed, the client merged with a competitor, and Greg's deal got thrown off the table as the merging company already had the IT infrastructure Greg was selling. Not long after, Greg became a finalist on another one and simply lost due to his competitor also having their best foot forward in the process. He lost fair and square, but he and his manager couldn't find anything they would have done differently during the postmortem review of the case. A few months later, he had another one he was about to get on the books and had no idea why it didn't end up going his way. It turned out that the buyer's wife used to work for Greg's company and thought they treated her unfairly when she left there. Unbeknownst to Greg, he didn't have a chance from the onset.

The weeks of no sales turned into months, and Greg's stock dropped fast in management's eyes. He was at the point where he didn't have time to revert back to the smaller accounts. It would have made him look bad to management, and he didn't have the pipeline of that size built anymore anyway. The young star of the future eventually was out looking for a new job.

When you work for yourself, you address issues like this as a strategist. When you work for somebody else, you are forced to worry about keeping your job rather than addressing the real issues. Which position would you rather be in?

CHAPTER 9

Remove Pawn from Your Business Card

Be extremely wary of promotions based on job titles and responsibilities. This is how companies motivate their employees, without costing them anything. This is also how culture and authority is created in offices, with limited impact on the bottom line of the owner, shareholders, or investors. Employees are a piece of a complex puzzle that has the goal of the business owners profiting as much as possible. Job title manipulation and hierarchy of title emphasis in an organization are strategies to take advantage of the pawns'—whoops, I mean *employees'*—emotions.

Joe was an area manager of client retention. Before he received that title, he was an account executive. He received a $6,000 raise and the new title in one year. Awesome! He had arrived! He should run and tell his parents and his girlfriend!

One time, a client asked Joe what "area" he was manager for; he shamefully had no answer. There wasn't a defined area. His title made no sense.

What's your title this year? What was it two years ago? If it's different now, did it make you happy when they put that on your business card? Did you like how the new title looked in the signature line of your e-mail? Did it make you feel good when you received this new title? That is *exactly* what your company had hoped it would do.

I am always impressed today as a business owner when I get called on by salespeople and notice the word "senior" on their business card before their title—Senior Sales Representative, Senior Account Executive, Senior Relationship Associate . . . whatever! Who cares? Nobody cares but the employee within the little culture that the company owner created to motivate him and his peers. If anything, I see it as a negative.

I would have more respect for the non-senior sales rep calling me because the non-senior person has more time to have the epiphany and not be employed at will any longer. Or maybe he already had the epiphany and doesn't really care about the money he is about to make from selling me something; he is seeing this instead as training. Ahhh, much respect to that non-senior person! If you have "senior"-something on your business card, nobody cares except you. Stop caring!

CHAPTER 10

How Much Does Your Company Make Off of You?

I was told once about a 12 percent raise I was getting. I was also told about a new fancy title I was getting another time. It's a joke. As pointed out in the previous chapter, I was a pawn. My title didn't mean anything, and the 12 percent increase wasn't as dramatic as it sounded when you looked at its impact on my paycheck. I'm glad I woke up and started preparing and seeing my workplace as training for my future. Is it unethical? Nope. I was a good employee making money for my company during the training process.

During your training, you must be a good employee. You need to keep your job in order to keep getting paid for this training. You need this time and experience to gain the knowledge and skills to be successful on your own. Make mistakes and fight the learning curve while working for someone else instead of going through that process and jeopardizing your future while you figure it out as a business owner.

Now, don't get upset when you actually do the math and figure out just how much your company is making off of you. If you are in an industry where there is no actual product but is more service oriented, the math is a little easier.

My most recent job was in this kind of position. I was bringing in from my client base about *$800,000* in consulting and brokerage fees annually. My compensation was about *$140,000*. Where was the *$660,000* going? Well, we had a fancy building and had support people. Figure my pro rata share of utility expenses and the building came out to, on the high end, $2,000 per month or *$24,000 a year*. Figure my assistant's salary was at $51,000 yearly, but she supported two other people as well . . . so that is *$17,000 a year* in expenses for my book of business. Figure my benefits and 401(k) match were about *$12,000 a year*. Lastly, let's figure my annual travel expenses and conference registrations came out to *$20,000 annually*, and that I had an additional *$10,000 per year* in expenses of miscellaneous items.

That comes out to $223,000 per year in expenses and my compensation, *leaving behind $577,000 to my employer.*

But wait! There was management and upper management that didn't have books of business that needed to get paid—my book of business must help support that, right? There is an HR department, a mail room, a custodial staff, an accounting department, an IT department, and a business office that are not tied into any book of business that all need to get paid. There are shareholders or investors that need dividends, and the company stock price has to go up as well.

What do any of these things have to do with me or my clients? Nothing! Does my client get better service because our CFO has a well-paid assistant or because our shareholders got paid dividends last quarter? Nope, our client gets good service because of me!

I know what you might be thinking right now: those non-revenue generating departments are still critical parts of an organization. Yes, they are. I work with HR departments for what my company provides, and I know *firsthand* the issues they have and the things they have to deal with; they are a very important piece of the corporate puzzle. The bigger an organization is, the more critical those pieces of the puzzle become. But guess what? THOSE DEPARTMENTS DO NOT HELP YOU BETTER SERVE YOUR CLIENTS!

Now, if you are on a team, it is trickier to evaluate how much your company is making off of you. Be honest with yourself and do your best to guesstimate the salaries and expenses of other team members you work with on your accounts. You should end up with net revenue going back to the company that is based on business you are working on. If you are newer in an organization, the company might not be making anything off of you . . . YET! Just wait until you become a "senior" employee.

If you are in an industry where there is an actual product being manufactured and not just a service, you need to do some diligence in figuring out what the real expenses are. Or if there is equipment necessary for performing a service, you need to take that expense into consideration.

I have a friend who is in management at a retail laser hair removal center. She makes six figures and never went to college. She is a personable and very good salesperson. She loves how much she makes, but she is starting to see the light. She knows that they pay their technicians an hourly wage to perform the service. She knows how much the equipment to do the service costs. She knows how much rent and utilities are for their location. She can work backward and figure out exactly what her company makes off of each of her sales.

When translating how much your company makes off of you to how much you can make on your own, you need to take into consideration any up-front costs. If capital is necessary for purchasing equipment or supplies, find out how much that would cost and what the loan payments would be each month from a bank. Later, I will discuss various strategies for addressing up-front money concerns.

When it's all said and done, collectively, your company is profiting from you being there. If they aren't, you won't be there for very long. Let them make money off of you, be a good employee, and take notes of how you are going to do things better at your own company.

When you start your own company after you complete your paid training, you won't be a complex organization on day one, and you won't have all that overhead. You can keep the majority of the revenue for important things . . . like taking better care of your clients and paying yourself.

CHAPTER **11**

Why Be Loyal to a Company Keeping You Down?

When I played football at Notre Dame, head coach Lou Holtz hired an assistant coach named Urban Meyer to be on his staff. The young, unproven Meyer, from day one, was a very well-respected member of the football staff.

It didn't take Meyer long to advance his career. He left Notre Dame for the head coach job at Bowling Green State University. Going from assistant coach to head coach is a big advancement. He was successful at Bowling Green and later on took another head coach job offer from the University of Utah. He was successful there as well and was then offered the same job at the University of Florida, where he went on to win two national championships and became one of the highest-paid college football coaches in the country.

I use him as an example because his career advancement was incredible: he moved up with each step and kept leaving his former employer behind (many college coaches, including

Lou Holtz, have similar advances on their way to their dream job). Meyer didn't work in an industry where it was possible to start his own company—it's not very realistic for him to create his own college football team. He made the most of the opportunities presented to him and climbed fast.

The funny thing is that it is acceptable in Meyer's business the way he did it. Each former employer he had expected him to leave after his success and didn't hold it against him. He was moving "up" each time. The head coaching job at Bowling Green is better than an assistant coach job at Notre Dame. The head job at Utah is better than Bowling Green, and the head coaching job at Florida is better than Utah. When he was winning at Utah and Bowling Green, his bosses knew he would be leaving eventually for a better job—his bosses didn't do anything to make his team lose to prevent those future and more desirable job offers. His industry has a hierarchy of football programs defined by history and the conferences they play in that make one job better than another. The administration of each college knows that it can't do much to stop a coach from leaving a lower-level school to take a job at a bigger one; it's more or less how the game works in college football.

Let's translate that now to the business world. It's not acceptable to do this, and no employer is going to expect or encourage their best employees to move on to bigger and better things with other organizations. They want that person to stay in their organization. The owners of mom-and-pop's cheese manufacturer are not hoping their top sales rep could go work for Kraft one day. Executives at Kraft are not hoping their top employees would figure out a better way to do things and then implement the idea on their own to directly compete with them. This only happens in places like college football.

Your boss and your company do not care about you. They only care about you as your position relates to their company, not what is ultimately best for you. So, guess what? You are the one that has to care, nobody else will. You are the one who has to care, nobody else will. (That was written twice for a reason.) You have to worry about what is best for you; your boss will only be looking out for you within the context of the company you are employed. Don't be naïve enough to think differently regardless of the sympathy card when your grandma died or the dinners out with spouses during non-work hours.

Isn't advancing your career better than being in the same position at the same company year after year? Of course it is, but your company doesn't want you to know it. In Meyer's case, his employer knew it each time and accepted it. Your company will not be training you for the next step, encouraging you to take it, or accepting it when you do it. It is on *you* to make the moves, it is on *you* to make it happen, it is on *you* to realize this is all training.

Forget loyalty to your current employer; he doesn't want you to advance. He wants you to stay an assistant coach and not take the head job. Maybe you feel as if you already have the head job at Bowling Green. When you start your own business, you'll have the head job at Florida. Your boss doesn't want you to be great and do great things for *you*, so why are you worried about loyalty to him?

I realize that the last three paragraphs probably came across as cynical. Of course you can have a personal relationship with your boss that is deeper than just your work. However, you truly are clueless if you believe that he or she is going to actively encourage you to seek other employment opportunities. That is, unless it would be a load off his shoulders if you quit as you are a low-performing employee anyway, or he is secretly conspiring against your employer.

If you are finding this too harsh or offensive, this is your wake-up call. Wake up!

Assuming your boss values his position at your company, he will always put the company ahead of you. The work you do is a reflection on him. Your leaving to go work somewhere else will make him look bad to his boss. (*"How could you let a top performer leave us!"*)

Your leaving that company to start your own operation and compete against them is not going to be something that will make your manager happy. It's not something he strives for you to do one day. You will never find yourself in a position where this is the case. It may seem like your boss has your best interests in mind, but at some level, there will always be the pull to keep you where you are in the organization you are already in. Why would you feel like you need to be loyal to these people?

Now, now, wait a minute . . . If you are all about "you" at your current place of employment, you won't have to figure out how to time up when you resign, instead you will be fired before it happens. When I say to be about "you," I am not telling you to be a bad employee or display this attitude open-ly. I am saying to have this attitude in terms of loyalty—do *not* let loyalty to people that have been good to you stop you from going on your own. Maybe they have been good to you in the course of your employment, but ultimately, they did that for the overall good of the company, not for the overall good of you.

Remember, you have this job for one reason . . . that is the paid training you are receiving. Don't let loyalty get in the way of that.

CHAPTER 12

Why Be Loyal to a Boss That May Leave You?

You don't need to have heard of Gary Barnett or care about who he is to follow my next point. It doesn't matter if you know him or not. His story illustrates a great point regarding loyalty.

The man took Northwestern University from having what many considered one of the worst Division 1 football programs in the land to one of the best. People everywhere jumped on the Northwestern bandwagon in the mid-1990s and were going crazy for Northwestern football under head coach Gary Barnett's leadership. Some of the best high school football players in the country were then suddenly choosing Northwestern University to play for Gary Barnett. With him, the story of Northwestern football becoming a big-time player, after years of losing, began.

The university and the city all embraced Gary Barnett; he was a celebrity. There was a restaurant named after him right off the campus. The applications for new students to the university skyrocketed because of how the football program was doing under him. He *was* Northwestern football, and people *loved* him for doing great things with the football program, the community, and the school.

The perceived "better" jobs at Notre Dame and UCLA opened up, and Barnett was an obvious candidate for those positions. He immediately took himself out of the mix and made it clear in the media that he was committed to Northwestern and wasn't interested in coaching anywhere else. The players loved it, the university loved it, and the community loved it. Northwestern not only had a great coach, but we knew he was *not* going to be leaving for another job somewhere else. It was great.

Then one day, the head coaching job at Colorado University opened up. Barnett is a Colorado native, and he took the job and put Northwestern in his rearview mirror. The leader of our organization just jumped ship on all the people that believed in him and committed to playing for him. The Northwestern players (employees) now had a new coach (manager/boss).

Barnett had it made at Northwestern; the man could have done no wrong. But he broke his loyalty and left.

Do you believe that your boss's loyalty to your company or to you is strong enough? Or do you feel, when a scenario that is better for him presents itself, he will take it like Barnett did? It's time for you to throw that loyalty out the door and worry about what is best for *you*.

CHAPTER 13

W-2 Employees Don't Get Rich

When I was still working for someone else, I would often do things that made me feel rich, even though I wasn't. At twenty-two, I had a Mercedes and put chrome rims on it (back when it was still cool to do so). At twenty-five, I bought a four-thousand-square-foot house with a subprime mortgage that was interest-only and amortized over forty years. I owned two Mercedes and a Jaguar. To have personal gratification or maybe earn notoriety among my peers, I was buying things to look rich.

I also remember the things I would look forward to, like holiday weekends and days off of work. I found myself constantly looking forward to vacations and was planning them many months in advance. I was an employee in Corporate America, and without realizing it, I was just running in place. I was not getting ahead.

"Rich" is a relative term. I live in downtown Chicago and have a very nice place. If I moved to the suburbs, my home would be nicer. If I moved to Malibu, it wouldn't be as nice.

If you make decent money and your friends are all teachers and public servants, then you feel rich. If you are the highest earner in your office or are considered well paid for your position and your age, you feel pretty good about your salary.

But, as an employee, you will never get paid as much as if you made it on your own. Overall, you will always be just one function of a moneymaking machine your employer has built to make other people rich (owners, shareholders, etc.). You will not become rich. You may think you are because you're making more than people in your office, but who is making more when you are in the owner's office? On the twentieth floor of my old job, I was pretty well paid. Up on the twenty-sixth floor, where the executives were, my compensation was laughable. I now make twenty-sixth-floor compensation on my own.

If you are a support person, or are in any type of non-sales or non-executive role, you can count on cost-of-living increases for the rest of your life. I know, I know, you can get promotions, and maybe you have already; go ahead and keep drinking that Kool-Aid. But wait, your boss is retiring next year and you are first in line for that position, drink away!

If you are in an organization that describes your salary increase in percentages, you are in bad shape if you ever want to make a lot more money. If you make $60,000 and your boss gives you a 20 percent raise, don't let him say 20 percent and how lucky you are. Make him say $12,000 per year, or $1,000 per month, or $700 or so after taxes each month. You aren't buying a yacht with your extra $700 . . . and you probably aren't going to be seeing many 20 percent increases anyway.

NON-SALESPEOPLE AND NON-EXECUTIVES: This may be a hard truth to swallow, but you will never make as much as the execs do, the same way you will never make as much as the top salespeople. One day, if you are lucky and after years of being underpaid, maybe you will become an exec yourself. Whoa! Hooray for you! Plan on working your rear end off to get there. And while you are working that rear end into shape, you are making money for somebody, assuming you are successful. If you aren't successful, you aren't getting the exec job.

Who's deciding if you are successful enough for the exec job? Not you, is it? Is it your boss, your manager, the president? Do you like somebody else controlling your life like this, employee?

If you are an executive, or on the track to becoming one, remember, "rich" is more than just money. Also remember that "executive" is a relative term. Are you an executive at a Fortune 500 company? You may become financially free, but are you in control of your destiny still? When you retire, do you have something to sell? Do you have real equity other than some stock options that may or may not be worth any-thing? Are you relying on your 401(k) match to make you rich down the road?

I don't know about you, but I would rather *not* wait until I am fifty-nine and a half to start enjoying life. Is that your plan, to wait to be rich at retirement?

If you start treating your job as a training ground, you will know when you are better than your employer and can do it better on your own . . . then you will see what big money really looks like and laugh at your previous self.

Business owners look at things differently. They aren't hoping for that raise or that promotion to increase their W-2 earnings; they are looking for ways to grow their business and are controlling their own fate in the process.

Section 3
Industry Evaluation

Now that you understand that you should at least consider working for yourself instead of making money for someone else, you now need to figure out if the paid training you are getting is the right kind of training.

This section will help you decipher whether starting a business in the industry you are in is a good idea or not. It will help you evaluate whether the product or service you offer is feasible to do on your own, whether or not you will be able to compete with the big guys on your own, and how long the industry you are in and the company you are going to start could possibly last.

If you are currently unemployed or in between jobs, your evaluation should center on your employment history as it would help you decide where to go from here.

<u>Caution:</u> This section may lead you to ponder whether or not the industry you are in today still makes sense for you.

CHAPTER **14**

Product vs. Service

If the basis of your current job is in a product-oriented business, you are going to have a little more to think about before you make your move versus working for a business that provides a service. Don't fret; it could still be done, but you need to add a step to your preparation.

If you are at a company that manufactures computers or grows palm trees, you may need to come up with capital to go out on your own. You might need the manufacturing capabilities to make the computers; that will take money. You will need land to grow the palm trees. There are ways to make it happen though, so do not let the lack of capital stop you because you just might not need any capital at all.

If you feel as if you work for an employer that is making money and you have the ability to do it better, then you can find a way to get it done even if your business is product oriented. One route is through finding investors, which I personally avoided at all costs. I didn't want to have to answer to investors, and I didn't want to ask friends for money. I was told that there is no way I can compete in the market I am in. In other words, there is no way I can get high-profile clients on my own, like I did with my former employer, if I didn't have the capabilities and value-added services companies like my former employer had. I didn't have the money to do this on my own internally, so I found another way . . . outsourcing!

My former employer of the same field had a compliance specialist, a legal consultant, an actuary, and other things that they used to flex their muscles and sell to clients as "value-added services" in working with them. I was in that selling process when I worked there, and I knew firsthand that there were a lot of smoke and mirrors with those non-mandatory items in the insurance brokerage business, and that the majority of the clients didn't need, care or ever utilize the services of these business units. However, how could I compete on my own for new business if I couldn't match these services in my presentation to prospective clients? Especially when so many of my competitors would highly emphasize their importance?

Many clients looked for those services to be available, even if they didn't think they would ever use them. I outsourced by setting up contracts with specialized firms that let me rent such services on a retainer or per-use basis. I was able to speak of their abilities in my sales presentations and gave my clients confidence that they were there if needed. I found a way to compete on my own, and it didn't cost me a thing in up-front capital.

Look at the industry that you are currently in and evaluate whether or not you can outsource anything. Would service suppliers be willing to let a small, start-up company—like the one you are going to start—access their services? (Make sure you find the right answer and don't be influenced by your Kool-Aid drinking peers.)

If your company is manufacturing a product internally, is it possible for you to manufacture and sell that same product by outsourcing some of the work? Maybe your up-front margins won't be as large as your former employer's, but you can still get there and do it as good or better. In a later chapter, I will discuss evaluating how competitive you can be in such situations. Almost everything can be outsourced.

I currently work with a firm that provides my company with advertising brochures and literature. I have come to be friends with the rep that handles our account. Over lunch one day, I asked him about their printing press and asked about turnaround time on some things I was thinking about having printed. I was surprised to hear that his answer was dependent on the workload of the printing press they send their work out to.

What! This brochure company didn't have their own printing press? In the three years that I worked with them, I was always under the impression that everything was done internally. Now I find out that they were a brochure company that was outsourcing their printing. They weren't doing anything but taking orders and going to an outsourced graphic designer and an outsourced printing press to give me my product. Then again, I have always received excellent service and competitive prices from them. I am their client, and I work with them because they are responsive and give me what I need. I don't care that they outsource things.

When it comes down to it, the client only cares about two things—the quality of the product and the quality of the customer service. You get new clients by being good at sales. The sales process is easier if you have a good product. You will retain your clients by providing good ongoing service. If you need to outsource some work in order to manufacture the widgets you are selling, you need to personally make sure that the quality is there.

It is your company's product that you are selling, not the product that is coming in externally from an outside manufacturer. Even though in actuality it may come from there, the client doesn't know it or care. Therefore, you need to make sure there is heavy-duty quality control on anything you outsource because at the end of the day, it is your product. Whether that's a farm you are getting feathers from to make the pillows you are selling or the tax advice given to your clients from the accounting firm you have retained, all the client knows is that the product he or she is buying is your company's. Make sure the quality is there in all facets when you outsource, and make sure it is worthy of putting your name on.

If you work for a business that provides a service, you can skip most of what preceded this paragraph—but not entirely. My work is service oriented, but I still needed to outsource to be competitive by bringing value-added services my competitors were offering to the table.

If you work for a service-oriented company (e.g., repair work, brokerage, stock trading, childhood education, recruiting, law, medical testing, really anything at all), you don't have to worry as much about the outsourcing component as you are not manufacturing anything. You just need to figure out if you are better than whom you would be competing against. Sure, you may need some equipment and you may need office space, stay in paid training until you are ready and have the means to do so. I suggest loans from a bank instead of investors.

My friend Ethan worked as a salesperson for a medical testing company. He was successful and was in an industry where going on his own was pretty easy because it was service oriented—at least easy for someone paying attention and learning from his paid training. The company he worked for would sell to doctors and outsource the testing to a local lab. He was able to not only go out on his own and outsource the testing to one of the many other labs in the area, he was also able to call on the same doctors that he had already developed relationships with at his old job.

Was this unethical? No. He decided to offer a slightly different kind of testing that didn't compete directly with his former employer's. He worked at his old job for three years, learned the business, and then went on his own with basically no expenses. He now has a salesperson under him making over six figures. Now his only worry is that this employee might have the same epiphany one day and do to him what he did to his former employer! That is a good problem to have.

Whatever you do, do not let the atmosphere at your work fool you into thinking that the little guy can't compete. The bigger the company you work for, the more you are going to hear things like that. People at such companies need to think things like that to protect their mental well-being and justify the choices they made for their lives.

Pay close attention to how things work and decide what can be outsourced and/or what can even be eliminated altogether. I knew that my old employer's full-time legal specialist, compliance specialist, and actuary were not relevant to the servicing of 99 percent of our clients. I also knew that there were plenty of firms out there that specialized in such services and could do it better and, best of all, were willing to outsource those services to people like me!

CHAPTER 15

Find the Service in the Product

You may work for a company where duplicating the manufacturing of your product or outsourcing the manufacturing or the value-added services is not an option. There are businesses where multimillion-dollar pieces of equipment are necessary. There are businesses that need major up-front money to even get noticed by a significant share of the marketplace.

I started my career working for a company that has governmental regulations in financial reserves they must have in order to exist. It was an insurance company. I couldn't quit my job and start my own insurance company; I would need tens of millions of dollars in order to make that work. There are many other businesses where the same would be necessary. I got onto a different side of the business in my second job, one that would make the path to going on my own much easier, with far less capital needed. It was the brokerage side of the business. I was already experienced in working with brokers as an insurance company sales rep.

Then I went and worked as a broker for a large insurance

brokerage firm. I learned the business well at both places, and I got trained there for what I am doing now. I was also successful at both places and generated for each of them significant revenue. Since I didn't have tens of millions of dollars, I knew that in order to capitalize off of my paid training, I needed to go the broker route.

Such parallels exist in any industry. If nothing else, there are always opportunities for specialized consultants. There are always opportunities similar to starting a brochure company and outsourcing the designing and printing. You have to keep your eyes open and find the opportunity.

Guy worked for a company as a sales rep selling IT services to hospital administrators. He knew he wanted to be a business owner and run his own show, but the job he had made it quite difficult to pull off on his own. For one, he didn't have the background to set up the IT infrastructure needed, and he didn't have the capital to hire someone to do it for him. (I'm not sure how much he evaluated the idea of outsourcing; maybe that could have worked.)

Instead, he saw an opportunity while calling these hospital administrators as a sales rep. He had some friends that were recruiters and headhunters, and he knew a bit about that business from talking to them. He thought of starting his own company that specialized in recruiting for physicians, and he would use all of his hospital administration contacts to make it happen. He found an opportunity to start a business with very little capital needed. He had an idea of a way to do it better than other recruiting firms by having the niche focus of just physicians. Without his paid training in becoming familiar with the culture of hospitals and physician groups, he would have never come across this opportunity. The light bulb would have never turned on. He partnered with someone that had a background in recruiting and his company was launched.

Matt does business line sales for a national Internet, phone, and cable company. He is content as an employee and makes good money. Due to the job he has, it's not even on his radar screen to start his own company. What's he going to do? He doesn't have the capital to develop an infrastructure for a company that could compete at this level; it's just not realistic. He needs to seek other avenues within that industry that do not require as much infrastructure or capital, switch jobs, get paid to learn at the new job, and then start his own company.

Matt may find that there isn't another side of his industry that can be started without deep capital. If his goal was to be a business owner and he concluded that he never could be in that industry without the capital, then he should switch industries and seek paid training elsewhere.

Ray works for a large national long-haul trucking and logistics company. His company acts as the middleman, getting paid for setting up the trucks with the businesses that need them. He needs to make sure the trucks are getting to where they are supposed to be and that they are constantly running. It's a business with a lot of moving pieces, and he is good at it. He told me about his plan to start his own company utilizing the contacts he has in place; he was confident that his business would be successful.

Ray's business plan called for $750,000 in capital to get started, and he didn't have it. So he told me he was attempting to bring in investors. I stopped him midsentence and asked him what the heck he needed that much money for. He then explained to me that he was going to buy his own trucks and run them with his new company. This was backward. He already knew the industry and worked for an intermediary brokering out the trucks that other people own. His plan was to take the next eighteen months in raising the capital to buy his own trucks and then quit his job and open up his company. Rather than waiting eighteen months to open a business with investors to answer to, how about opening it tomorrow with nobody to answer to?

Like I said though, Ray is good at what he does and knows his business. He is the one with the paid training in that industry, not me. So there is probably a method to his $750,000 madness that I don't see. I wouldn't recommend going that route though.

It's not always an easy task to find this path. Just remember your options: outsourcing, getting a loan, moving to a side of your industry that makes more sense for going on your own one day, or switching industries altogether. Give it deep thought and evaluate whether or not it is realistic to do in the job you currently have.

CHAPTER **16**

What's the Big Guy Doing?

In many aspects of life, perception is not the same as reality. I have observed this to be the case in the business world when it comes to evaluating competition in a particular industry. It is utterly important to identify the reality of your ability to get new clients as you evaluate your decision, and not fall victim to just immediately buying into how things seem. Let me make this point with a direct correlation to what I experienced in deciding where to play football in college.

After high school, I decided to attend Notre Dame on a football scholarship. It was 1995, and schools like Michigan, Florida, Nebraska, Stanford, and many others were all offering me full scholarships as well.

I also had an offer from Northwestern University. It was the closest of all the schools to my home, and I liked their academics and their coaching staff. There were many reasons to go there, but the issue was that they hadn't been good in football for many years. Their coach kept telling me that I have a chance to be a part of something special, something that is going to be huge, and something that is going to shock everyone. But I just couldn't buy into it. How could Northwestern, who hasn't been good at football in decades, be better than these other football powerhouses I had scholarship offers from? There is no way they could be. I decided to go to Notre Dame over all the others.

I was a young eighteen-year-old believing perception over fact in choosing a college to play football at. Very similar to what many forty-year-olds are buying into in terms of their career choices in the business arena.

In my first game as a college football player at Notre Dame, ironically, we played Northwestern and were heavy 28-point favorites going into the game. Northwestern beat us and went on to have a season that made college football history.

Northwestern wasn't supposed to be better than Notre Dame; it didn't make any sense that they won the game.

When the start-up operation with a handful of employees beats the firm with 45 locations and 7,000 employees, people wonder "how did that happen?"

Two years later, the Notre Dame head coach I went to play for (Lou Holtz) resigned from his position, and I decided to transfer due to that and some other reasons. Again, I had options of many traditional football powerhouses. I narrowed down my search to Miami, UCLA, Wisconsin, and Northwestern. Northwestern had only been considered good for the last two years at that point, and many thought of it as a short-lived fluke. I transferred to Northwestern anyway, and many critics thought it was a bad move from a football standpoint, explaining there is no way they could be good consistently and that they only "got lucky" the last two seasons.

At twenty years old, I was intelligent enough to pose the question, "Why not?" I wasn't going to make the same mistake twice, the same mistake that many fifty-somethings keep making in the business world as they move from job to job throughout their career. The National Collegiate Athletic Association heavily regulates how many scholarships a football program can offer, how many coaches it can have, and how many times a week it can practice. The other schools had to play with eleven guys on the field at a time, just like Northwestern. People, with their short memories, said, "Why would you leave Notre Dame for Northwestern?" even though Northwestern just beat Notre Dame the last time they played. Yet, people still didn't get it.

When you start your business, all that matters is that you win. It doesn't matter if it *seems* like someone else is better than you or if it *seems* like the competition can easily beat you. All that matters is who actually wins.

I got what other people didn't get. I saw no reason why Northwestern couldn't compete against Notre Dame and the other schools. The other schools did not have any type of competitive advantage over Northwestern. There was no fundamental factor that would make one team better than another.

It was all perception. A competitive advantage would be that the other teams got to have more players or more coaches. There was no actual competitive advantage, only the perception that the other schools (including Notre Dame) were better—even when Northwestern was beating them.

For the next fifteen years, Northwestern consistently outperformed Notre Dame in football. There were people out there that still thought Notre Dame was better though. However, perception was *not* reality.

If the business you are in is dominated by some big players, you need to evaluate why those players are the big players. Is there something better that they can offer? Do they have a competitive advantage over you if you started your own company? In other words, do they get to play with twelve players on the field versus your eleven?

For the business I am in, the answer is no. As insurance brokers, we all access the same premium rates from the insurance companies we work with; in other words, pricing was not going to be a competitive advantage. There are "value added" services that can be brought to the table, but I found a way to duplicate those through outsourcing when I first started out, thus leaving my bigger competitors with no competitive advantage over me.

A competitive advantage is something tangible that will give the client a better product or service. A competitive advantage is *not* how long a company has been in business, how many locations it has, or how many employees it has. Those things might be perceived values, but they are not competitive advantages. If a competitor has fifty locations and ten thousand employees, so what? What about that translates into a better product or service for the client?

In the 2000s, there was a phenomenon of celebrities being famous for being famous. Think about it: what made Paris Hilton famous? She was famous because she was famous. Are the biggest players in your industry the best because of an actual reason, or does everyone just say they're the best? Or are they getting attention because they have a competitive advantage over others—a tangible competitive advantage that allows them to actually serve the client better by delivering a higher-quality product or service?

At one of my old jobs, the Kool-Aid was drunk all over the place in sales presentations. We would pitch how long the company has been around for and how many employees we have, as well as how many locations there are. One day, a client asked me how that was going to make me do a better job for him than somebody else.

He was right, there was no reason it was going to. It was not a competitive advantage. The bigger the company you work for, the more you are going to hear about how bigger is better within your organization. You will have sales literature talking about your company's size; you will have the number of locations on your website. Unless you can attach that to why it is better for a client, it is not a competitive advantage.

My company now competes with the biggest brokerage firms. I am talking about national, publicly traded companies who have been around for fifty years and have thousands of employees. I beat such firms regularly. I have high-profile clients that they would love to have and try to get. Employees at such companies, after being beaten by me and my smaller, newer company, will call it a fluke or will say I got lucky. As they try to create and cling to that perception, because they are afraid of the reality, I will just keep winning—like Northwestern did.

Figure out if the bigger players in your industry really have a competitive advantage. Come up with a way to beat the biggest in your industry and then just do it and don't talk about it to anyone except prospective clients. Let your competitors in the marketplace think you aren't even there or that you don't matter. Quietly get new clients and take their clients while flying under the radar screen. Let them all think you don't matter as your business continues to grow at their expense.

Now, there are and always will be industries in which there are competitive advantages for the big guys. One of my favorite TV shows of all time is *The Office*. If you haven't seen it, I highly encourage you to. It's hilarious. The premise of the show is based on a sales office of a fictional paper supply company called Dunder Mifflin. An underlying theme in the early seasons of the show is that the employees are in constant worry about the bigger players in their industry (i.e. Staples or Office Depot) buying them out or putting them out of business. There are incidences where it is revealed that they cannot get their paper for as low a price as the bigger players get it for. As a result, the client is able to pay less for the same product if they go to one of the big guys instead of the much smaller Dunder Mifflin. This *is* a competitive advantage. There is a tangible benefit to the client by going to the bigger competitor.

If I go to a casino and I play blackjack, and if I play it perfectly using the strategies that will give me the best odds, the casino still has a competitive advantage over me—even if I do everything right. No matter what, the odds are in their favor. I will eventually lose because of the advantage my competitor (the casino) has over me.

Do not start a company if you have competition that innately can bring better quality for the same price or the same quality for a lower price than your company can bring to the client. Your clients will figure it out, and you will not last very long. If you are starting a company where there are options for your clients that are better, much like gambling at a casino, you will eventually lose because your competition has an advantage over you.

Be honest with yourself about your current job and the industry you are in. Look at it as impartially as possible. Do not let "perceived" values to a client stop you; focus only on *real* competitive advantages that others may have on the much smaller company you want to start. If you find that there are competitive advantages that cannot be overcome, you need to take a step back and evaluate if this is the right industry to launch a business in.

NOT Competitive Advantages: Years in business, number of employees, number of managers, locations, locations of managers, number of clients.

Real Competitive Advantages: Anything resulting in lower cost or better quality to the client.

"Our company has over eighty years of experience," said the corporate sales rep to the client.

"Do you, personally, have eighty years of experience that is going to make you service my account better?" responded the unimpressed client.

CHAPTER **17**

Market Share

Some friends and I were throwing around ideas about some "side" businesses to start. Nothing that we were going to get rich or make a huge living off of; just something on the side that would be fun to do and would put a little money in our pockets. I threw at them the idea of starting a limousine service. My one buddy said, "What are you going to do to make it different or better than the existing limo services?" My answer was, "Nothing."

I didn't start the limousine service, but from what I could tell about it in the limited research I did do was that the start-up costs were not too high and that there was a lot of demand for limousines. There were a lot of limo companies already out there too. But, again, the conversation wasn't about us getting rich or anything; it was just for fun and a few extra bucks. The intent was to just take a little slice of an industry that clients have a lot of demand for already in Chicago. That's it. We weren't creating a market; the idea would have been just to get our piece of the existing pie.

The same line of thinking is true for my insurance broker-age firm. My insurance brokerage firm is my main source of income, so I am obviously not going to try and be mediocre or just strive to be average. I am constantly looking for ways to improve and bring new and valuable things to our clients. The point is that I knew the industry I was in had a *lot* of busi-ness. It is the selling of employee benefits—that means every employer that purchases 401(k) plans, health insurance, den-tal insurance, life insurance, disability insurance, and many other benefits for its employees is part of the market. There are many employers offering benefits out there, and they are all potential clients. I did not start my company thinking I was going to put my former employer out of business. I didn't need to. All I wanted was a piece of the market that already existed.

When you are evaluating the industry you are in, pay close at-tention to the customer base that exists, as well as its potential customers. In order for you to make money with your com-pany, do you have to potentially put somebody else out of business? If so, who are you better enough than to do that to?

If the market you are in is gigantic, but with only few players, you need to have a plan on how you would be able to enter that and succeed.

If the market you are in is gigantic with many players, you can more easily slip in and just start taking your own clients without too much disruption to the rest of the industry. This is what I did.

If the market you want to be in does not currently exist, make sure there isn't a reason for it not existing and that you do, in fact, have something desirable to offer. This is huge; if you have an idea for something that you think is extraordinary and that doesn't exist yet, make sure that there are buyers for it prior to proceeding. Good ideas are not always necessarily going to translate to good businesses.

Look very closely at the marketplace when deciding if the paid training you are getting is in an industry where going on your own makes sense and remember that you don't necessarily need to put your current employer out of business in order to succeed.

CHAPTER 18

Longevity

Over the years, we have seen many video rental spots close down. Web-based services, on-demand cable, and other technological advancements have moved on-site video rental outlets inch by inch toward obsoleteness. In the 1980s and 1990s, there were independently owned, mom-and-pop video rental stores all over the place. Where are they now?

Politicians often talk about the government taking over health care in America; there are plans that have gone to Congress, and many states have developed their own rules. What if one day the government gives everyone health care for free? If that happens, not too many people will be buying health insurance . . . you don't need to insure something that is free, do you? If this happens, it will have a major adverse impact on the industry I work in and put many firms like mine out of business.

I do have a plan for this circumstance but will have to kill you if I tell you it. Sorry, I can't give my competitors this roadmap by writing it in this book.

As you evaluate whether or not the industry you are in makes sense or not, you need to look very closely at the longevity of the industry. Is it going to exist in five, ten, or twenty years? Are there technological advancements, government regulations, or international competition that threatens to make the industry obsolete? It won't always be black and white when you evaluate the longevity of your industry, but you do need to be as impartial as you possibly can. You need to anticipate what might happen down the road and not just base your predictions on what has happened in the past.

Another part of the longevity conversation is your company itself. Even if your industry is not going away, do you have a plan that will make your company compete long term in it? Here are some questions to ask yourself:

- Are you going to be able to keep up with the times and the advances of your industry with your own company?

- Are you going to be able to offer a service or product that is desirable in the long term?

- Are you going to be able to sustain the price points to keep your clients happy?

I recall the episodes of *The Office* when the manager of the branch was no longer employed there. He went and started his own company and named it the Michael Scott Paper Company, after himself. It was a funny few episodes that consisted of the former manager calling his former clients at Dunder Mifflin and trying to sell them paper for cheaper prices. He used price as his value proposition to get them as clients to his new company. The problem was that he did not have access to paper for cheaper prices than his old company. He could find short-term success landing these accounts, but there is no way his pricing was going to be sustainable to carry on long term.

Ask yourself the following questions when evaluating longevity:

> » Is the industry you are in the on-site video retail rental business?

> » Is your company the Michael Scott Paper Company?

If you answered *no* to both of those, you may be in a business that has a chance.

Section 4
Self-Evaluation

This section will force you to take a look at yourself. Remember that this is not a "rah-rah" motivational book that is supposed to make you feel good. The purpose of this book is to guide you into using your current employment or future employment for one reason and one reason only—paid training.

This section is going to focus on the evaluation of you. While you consider starting your own company, you need to make sure you have the depth and competence to succeed in the business you are in. You are then determining if you have received enough paid training and if you are cut out to be a business owner.

If you were looking for a feel-good, you-can-do-it book . . . by now you should have realized that you bought the wrong book.

CHAPTER 19

Are You as Important as You Think You Are?

Corey quit his job at his employer to start up his own operation. He thought he was underpaid and, like me, was also in the insurance brokerage industry. He worked for a big employer and had success there for many years. When he went on his own, he was a big flop; he couldn't write any business. He would blame it on his non-compete agreement with the former employer, saying that it was tying him down.

After the two-year non-compete expired, guess what? He still couldn't write any business. He shut down his company and went crawling back with his tail between his legs, trying to get his old job back.

He made a mistake—a big one—during his paid training process and his evaluation of himself before he left his employer. He was a producer, selling brokerage and consulting services to clients as an employee of his former employer. The problem was he was doing too much selling of the company and not of himself. He would constantly emphasize the size and rich history of the organization—just like he was brainwashed to do as an employee there. When it came down to it, that was all he knew how to sell. When he went out on his own, he didn't know how to create any kind of value proposition that could differentiate him from his competitors.

Corey had banked on his former customers running to him after the non-compete agreement was up, and he also was banking on endorsements from various trade groups and organizations he worked with that he had successfully achieved in the past. He found out the hard way that nobody cared about him; they bought from him before because of the company he was selling. To the client, they were a client of that company, and he was an employee there that worked with them. If he left that company, in the client's eyes, he could be replaced—which is exactly what happened—and they all stayed with his former employer.

In the client's eyes, will the world stop if you disappear? What are *you* bringing to the table? During your self-evaluation, you need to determine why you are successful: are you currently selling you or the company you work for?

Have you ever heard someone that recently lost a job say things like, "The management had no idea how to run a company" or "They don't know what they want over there, they are so unstable"? These are excuses and are a way for a non-essential person to justify why he got fired or demoted.

You need to determine if you are essential to your clients or if as soon as you leave, somebody can just step right in and take your place. You also need to determine if the company can be run just as well without you—from the clients' standpoint, not yours.

Don't allow yourself to believe "it's office politics" why you didn't get the promotion or the raise. Perhaps it very well might be, but rather than just immediately assuming "it's politics," also consider that it may be because you don't deserve it. Or maybe it's because you are terrible and you are kind of delusional about what you are really bringing to the table. Why would management not see you as the star you are if you deserve it?

One of the worst things you can do is make an emotional decision to quit your job and go into business for yourself right after getting passed up on a promotion. Instead of pointing the finger, point the thumb and evaluate if you are really as good as you think you are.

During your paid training, evaluate how essential you are to your clients and to the organization. Be honest with yourself and do not make excuses or justify it if you are not. If you are not essential to your organization, you have not achieved success there and may not be able to on your own, yet. Consider that it may make sense to continue your path in paid training prior to going out on your own.

To run a business, you need to be able to be a success. You need to prove to yourself that you are able to do this as part of the process prior to starting your company. This is not always the case; you may have discovered something or stumbled across an idea that may accelerate you to go on your own prior to achieving success while still being under your employer. You do need to have an honest answer, though, to the question of "Why am I not successful here?" The answer to that question should help you figure out if you are ready or not.

If there is a valid reason for not being a success, it's okay. If you do not have a reason for not being prosperous, then you need to determine if you will be able to be on your own and know exactly how to do so. However, take note of the difference between a valid reason and an excuse. Things like office politics, unfair nepotism, or bad management typically fall in the excuse column.

Determining if you are ready or not really depends on the job you have and what industry you are in. There is no exact definition. What I suggest you do is look at yourself and compare yourself to others in your company and others in your industry with similar positions. Then ask yourself these questions:

1) Are you better than them?
2) Do clients think you are better than them?
3) Does your boss think you are better than them?
4) Why or why not?

CHAPTER 20

Categorize Your Experience Level

If you are in sales, this chapter is aimed at you. If you are not in sales, you should still take away the lessons being promoted within it as you figure out how you will be marketing your product.

There are four concepts I'm going to describe in this chapter. You may have heard various descriptions or definitions of these; below are mine:

- Inside Sales

- Outside Sales

- Order Taker

- Inferior Product Sales

Inside Sales

An inside salesperson is a person that is given prospects. This could be from potential customers calling in or from a book of business that he or she is supposed to upsell. I do not care if this person is able to leave the office and go visit potential customers. If that person is given warm leads, then he or she is inside sales.

Outside Sales

An outside salesperson is out knocking on doors, opening new accounts, and finding the money. The outside salesperson isn't given prospects to work; he or she needs to find them.

Order Taker

An order taker (my definition) is an inside or outside sales rep that is selling a product that is so desirable; not much convincing is necessary when getting a new client. The clients are going to buy it regardless.

Inferior-Product Sales

An inferior-product salesperson is selling a product or service that isn't perceived to be as good as its competitors' throughout the marketplace.

If I were to hire a new salesperson tomorrow for my company, I would hire somebody that has found success as an inferior-product salesperson. I would never hire an order taker. The problem is that many order takers think they are good salespeople, and maybe they could be, but it's not going to be demonstrated with an order-taking job. The problem is that most order takers do not realize that they are selling something that is guaranteed to be bought; their organization might not realize it either.

Case in point: my company often places insurance coverage with Blue Cross Blue Shield. They are a very strong player and are necessary. My clients utilize my services to make recommendations, consult, and place the insurance coverage with the appropriate insurer. I have sales reps from insurance companies calling on me to attempt to get me to put my clients with their companies. I get calls regularly from Aetna, Cigna, UnitedHealthcare, and Humana sales reps. My Blue Cross sales rep rarely, if ever, calls on me. However, more of my clients are with Blue Cross than any other insurance carrier. When I want to place a new client with them, I make a phone call and the sales rep takes the information and writes a new piece of business.

He is technically in outside sales, but he is never in my office. He thinks he is in outside sales, his company pays him like a person developing new business, and he gets rewards for making quotas, like an annual trip to their "conference meeting." However, he is an order taker, the reason being that Blue Cross has such an advantage over their competitors in particular regions that business will go their direction no matter what their sales reps do.

Don't get me wrong; my representative at Blue Cross is a very smart guy and is highly successful. I'm not making the point that order takers are bad. I also do not use the term "order taker" as an insult; I use it for what it means. If you are an order taker, you have not had to learn to sell at the level you will need to when you go into business on your own. You might think you are in sales, but how successful would you be if you didn't have the competitive advantages you have?

Order takers right now are getting annoyed as they read this, thinking to themselves that that is their job—to accentuate their positive features and competitive advantages. Yes, correct! That is what sales is! I am saying you are an order taker if people are seeking you out and you get business without doing any selling. If you are at a company like Blue Cross, people will come to it regardless—with or without you.

Are you currently in an order-taking job?

When you start your own business, you will need to have a way to sell. If you are counting on yourself to sell the product, that is great and exactly what I would recommend. However, you need to realize that you are not just taking orders anymore. Evaluate if you are an order taker or not by asking yourself the following questions:

- Does the company I currently work for have a huge competitive advantage over everyone else?

- Can I duplicate this competitive advantage in my own company?

- If I didn't exist in my company, would clients still go running there?

Martin works in sales at a large computer supplier that has a *huge* presence in Chicago. He was one of the original forty employees working there and, as a salesperson, has reaped the benefit of stock grants and a very nice income. He is in inside sales, but he calls it outside sales. He was given accounts in a territory, and it was his job to keep getting business out of them. This is a very important job for the company, and Martin has been successful doing it for years and has been making well over six figures for quite some time, in addition to the stock grants and other perks. If Martin wanted to start his own company, he wouldn't have the sales background that translates into what he will need to be doing. He is not going to maintain existing accounts or make sure current clients keep coming back—he will have to go find the clients in the first place, which is a lot tougher to do. He quite possibly would be very good at it; however, the success at his current position doesn't translate into ensuring that.

Samantha used to work for a big home developer in Chicago called Pulte. She got the job out of college, and her duty was to work in the trailers at new subdivision sites that were being developed. Her job was to work with the customers as they walked in asking for information about the subdivision. She would be the person to make the sale and would upsell things like upgraded countertops, finished basements, and dual vanities in the bathroom once the customer committed to buying the house. She made very good money for a person in her early to mid-twenties. Again, however, her sales experience at Pulte would not translate into what she would need to do in starting a business on her own. Samantha's job gave her a huge advantage. She would either need to address if her sales skills were good enough to do something much more difficult or evaluate if she could create the same streamline of customers coming to her at her own organization.

My Blue Cross sales rep, Martin, and Samantha all have good jobs and play important roles in their organization. They are all hardworking, intelligent, and motivated. None of their sales experiences would translate into how they would need to sell if they had their own business though. This is not to say that they would be incapable of it; they would just need to understand the differences and what would be necessary to succeed. It would be a harder job. You need to make this same determination in comparing what you do now versus what you would need to be doing on your own.

At my first job out of college, my company competed with other insurance companies like Blue Cross. Our product was perceived by most clients to be inferior. We didn't have the service capabilities, we didn't have the doctors and hospitals in our networks that our competitors had, and last but not least, our prices were higher. However, I am glad this was my first real job as it taught me how to sell. I had to be convincing to get someone to buy a product that perceptually wasn't as good for more money. There were some clients that it would be a good fit for; my job was to find those clients and make them understand why. We did not advertise, and unless they heard it from our sales reps, clients didn't know who we were.

I needed to promote our product, find potential clients, and convince them to buy a product that was considered by most to be inferior to other options in the market. When I went on my own, I had sales experience that directly translated to what I would need to do. My mind-set was that if I was able to do it with an inferior product, I should be able to do it at my own company with a superior product—which is what I believe I had put together.

On paper, when I started—and still the case today—there are competitors that appear to be superior from a traditional point of view. I have to accentuate what is brought to the table by working with my company and, most importantly, why it is better for the client.

Review your experience and figure out if it translates to what you will need to do on your own to get new business. Do not let your success or the money you make cloud your judgment. Remember Samantha, Martin, and my Blue Cross rep? All are very successful but do not have any of the sales experience that would translate into what they would need to do on their own. If they did decide to start a business, they need to take into consideration the much-harder sales process than what they have been used to. Look at yourself and evaluate what your current scenario is. Being successful at a big organization does not mean that you can do the same thing at your own in the future, especially when clients or prospects are being handed to you currently.

Below is some advice as you consider staring your own company; figure out which of these applies to you:

If you aren't in sales, you are diving into unknown territory as you will need to sell your product or service. If you don't plan on doing the selling, you will need a feasible plan. If you plan on hiring a salesperson, make sure he isn't an order taker.

If you are in inside sales, you need to recognize that it's more outside sales with a start-up business. Can you do that?

If you are an order taker, you probably sell a lot and enjoy it. You are successful and feel good about yourself. Considering you won't be able to just take orders when you go solo, how are you going to create that same streamline with your new company?

If you are an inferior-product salesperson or in outside sales, that's good—but only if you have been successful at it.

CHAPTER **21**

Look Around—Is Anyone Better Than You?

Take a look around your office: are you as good as the person sitting next to you? Are you better than everyone in your office? Are you better than everyone you have encountered at other branches of your organization? If you are not, you need to be before you go on your own.

These people are your future competitors. If not them personally competing against you when you go on your own, it will be people like them. It will be seasoned sales professionals in billion-dollar organizations that have been in business for decades. It will be "senior" salespeople making good money with more ammunition behind them in terms of the heritage of their organization. That is who you need to beat. You better make sure you are better than them before you go on your own; otherwise, it will be like David and Goliath, except in this story, Goliath is the one with the slingshot.

I recall a situation where an unsuccessful sales rep in my industry left the company he worked for to start his own. It was laughable, and nobody even cared. He was living in fantasy-land and thought he was better than he really was and that he was really just getting screwed by his employer when he kept getting passed up on promotions. The fact of the matter was that he wasn't as good as his peers, and when his peers became his competitors, he couldn't beat them. Needless to say, his business didn't last, and he is now back working for someone else with no control of his future.

You don't necessarily have to be the best person to have ever done the job you have in order to succeed as a business own-er. It really depends on what the business you are in is. If you are looking to gain a piece of an existing market and just win "your share" of the accounts that are out there, then you should look at the people around you differently. If you are concerned that Tom down the hall is a better salesperson than you are and he would be tough to beat all the time, ask yourself if you think you would beat him half the time. You don't need to put your current employer out of business, but you definitely need to have the ability to win your fair share of times if you are going to survive.

When you evaluate yourself versus your peers at your com-pany, remember to focus only on what matters. Be careful not to let the company Kool-Aid influence your evaluation. For example, if Joyce is the top account manager in your office because she has the biggest book of business, don't let the size of her book of business distract you from what it is you are evaluating. You are evaluating your abilities versus hers. You are evaluating what you are able to do for a client versus others.

Books of business at larger organizations often elevate some-one to a higher level in the hierarchy of perception in that company. But the reality is that sometimes a person's large number of clients just happens by mistake, and attrition of other account managers or shifting of territories grows some-body's client list. Remember to really evaluate your capabilities against that of everyone else—the tangible, real capabilities that will be important to clients, not what the company Kool-Aid has led others to believing is important.

A good place to start in this evaluation would be to look at things from your clients' point of view. If you left the company, would they see your replacement at that company as good, bad, or indifferent?

CHAPTER 22

Moving Backward

When I was twenty-five years old, my W-2 was right around $140,000. When I was twenty-six, it was around $87,000. I was better at what I was doing, in a great job, and had a lot of success and momentum going for me. The $53,000 pay cut came as a result of leaving one job for another. It was a critical move that I am glad I made. It got me to where I would later be in life.

However, I am ashamed to say that it wasn't this foresight that made me do it—it was actually the industry Kool-Aid. Nonetheless, the move panned out for me in the long run.

It was a big title at a great company with a relatively high base salary (but not-so-great total compensation plan). The respect of peers in the industry for getting the position was rampant, and my family was impressed as well. The fact of the matter was that I was going to be taking a huge step backward financially. Most salespeople in their twenties are trying to move up each year with W-2 income, but this move set me back two years to get to where I already was at my old job.

Why did I do it?

I did it for the respect and the title from the Kool-Aid I was drinking in my messed-up industry. It was a decision that goes against the core of this book, but it was a mistake that turned out great for me in the end.

Had I not taken that position as a broker/consultant/intermediary at that brokerage house, I would have more than likely continued working as a sales representative for insurance companies. Had I done that, I would have never have had the confidence (from lack of paid training) to make the leap into starting my own brokerage house. And it wouldn't have been feasible to launch my own successful insurance wholesaler. (There are too many reasons to list why that wouldn't have flown.)

As I look back at this chain of events, I encourage you to not be scared to take a step backward financially during your paid training process. If you do see your end game being a business owner, you must look at your career decisions with the big picture in mind. Don't evaluate jobs based strictly on how much you are going to make. Judge the jobs based on how they are going to teach you what you need to know. Look at the elements of the industry that they are going to expose you to.

When you start making decisions with this end game in mind, you will gather the knowledge and confidence you will need to be your own boss. Not to mention a little bonus: When you actually decide to make the move to go on your own, it's an easier decision if you aren't highly compensated at the job you are about to quit.

I jest with that last sentence, but there is some truth to it. I do recommend you make as much money as you can during your paid training—just don't let it hold you back. And don't let higher pay supersede why you would want to take one job over another if the other job would have been a better training ground for you.

Remember the big picture and where it is you desire to be in the future. If your desire is to be a highly paid employee and be controlled by someone, ignore this chapter.

CHAPTER 23

Differentiation and Price Cutting

Even when you are in an industry where you are just trying to get a slice of the existing market with your own company, you still need to have a plan and some type of value proposition that sets you apart. When I left my old employer to go on my own, my plan was to focus on a very specific niche and type of client to service. My idea was that this focus would bring a higher degree of comfort to new clients in working with me, knowing that all I do is work with similar clients with similar needs, wants, and issues. This niche focus is a differentiator for my firm and sets us apart from most of our competitors who tend to work with all clients regardless of the size or type of business they are in.

You do not have to have a niche, but you have to have something that makes you more attractive to clients over your competition—you have to have a reason for clients to want to do business with you. Unfortunately, a smaller, newer company doing the same thing as the bigger, established company offering the same value proposition is not going to be a great "story" in your sales pitch. Be different; come up with a plan for your prospective clients . . . a better one.

I could have *easily* not gone the niche route or created this value proposition. I probably could have been successful without it and won my fair share of times when competing for new business. However, at that point, it would have just been a crapshoot and I would be depending solely on my sales skills to win—basically hoping that a client likes me better than the other guys. With my niche focus, I know that when I am in a competitive situation, I have something that my competitors don't. I'm not relying on just sales skills; I am demonstrating some services and resources that my firm has available for clients that are not readily available elsewhere. It is a competitive advantage that I have in a specific market. Think hard, you will find something in your industry.

When figuring out your differentiator, please be more creative than price! Believe me, this will kick you in the rear end at some point; and if you get a client on lower prices, you will lose the client to lower prices in the future (that's Sales 101, my friend). Having said that, if you have a creative way to obtain a deliverable for a client at a lower rate—through negotiating, bargaining, or what not—then that is okay. But if you are just cutting fees to win and differentiate, that is not okay.

Take real estate agents for example: the going rate to sell your house is a 5 percent commission in Chicago. I see some realtors promoting themselves to do it for 4 percent or even less at times. Everyone knows the going rate is 5 percent, but these guys come out and offer the service for less. Basically, what those realtors are telling clients is that they do not have enough of a value proposition to differentiate themselves at even the going rate. They are cheapening themselves and telling clients they aren't better, or even as good, and that they need to charge less to justify working with them. They are turning themselves into a commodity. This is a weak, weak differentiator that ultimately puts you down in the clients' eyes.

Adversely, if a realtor is offering a value proposition in addition to the lower price, then it *might* work. Something like, "We give you excellent, personal service that you cannot find at the bigger, national real estate firms. We work from our homes with far less overhead, but still have all the same tools and even a greater personal touch. Because of our lower overhead and our higher-than-normal referral rate, we are able to offer our clients a rate of 1 percent less commission versus our larger competitors."

The reason I said it *might* work and not *will* work is because the client has to see the value proposition as real and of value—otherwise, it sounds like the realtor just can't compete at the going rate. In the above example, the value proposition might be so saturated among others in the market that it really isn't considered a differentiator at all to most clients.

Mike Gandy, whom I played football with at Notre Dame, had a great career in the National Football League and started in the Super Bowl one year. He told me a bit about how sports agents work and what their compensation is, as well as what kinds of experiences he has had dealing with them. He said he would get calls from agents other than his own quite regularly, attempting to get him to sign on with them. The agent that he works with gets a standard commission on whatever his earnings are. I pointed out that that is a lot of money out of his paycheck and asked if he ever gets calls from other agents offering to do it for less. He said he does sometimes, and he immediately hangs up on them because every player in the NFL knows those are inferior agents. He used a great line when he explained it to me by saying, "Price only matters in the absence of value."

Now, realize you might see some short-term success with rate cutting and you may attract some clients. In the long term though, these are not desirable clients. Note that big companies do it too, not just little guys trying to get started. No matter who is doing it, it is wrong and a bad way to practice your business. You are selling yourself short, and you are attracting clients that you don't want.

I had a situation during my fourth year in business where I was going after a high-profile client—a school in Chicago. A very large competitor was also going after this client, and we were the two finalists for their business. When the competitor found out that it was my company on the other side, and when it looked like the business was going to go my way, my competitor cost us all money. Not because they are stupid people that don't like making money, but because they started assuming.

From the company Kool-Aid they were drinking, their representatives assumed that the only way a client like this would work with a much smaller company like mine is if I am offering to do it for less money. I was actually proposing to do it for more money to my firm than they were proposing.

The prospective client put us up against each other, and we had a series of meetings following each other, with the client asking us questions about things the other finalist said.

Then in the last meeting, they asked me if I would lower my prices. Now mind you, the prices were already cut down by both sides on something that you typically would not bring your price down on. They asked me if I would lower it to an amount that didn't make any sense for the amount of work that had to be done—the requested pricing would essentially have my team and me working for close to minimum wage. I answered no and stated that we couldn't do it for that price. They told me that my competitor has offered to do it for that price though and we would need to match their revised offer. I told them they should just keep having these meetings and eventually it will be free.

The client was putting us in a nonstandard position and basically just having us go back and forth to get their business with lower pricing. I played the game for one round but stopped at a level just above a number that would make the case undesirable to even have on the books. My competitor, however, didn't flinch and kept dropping their price. This is an undesirable client; if my business was filled with clients like this, I would hate my job and make very little money.

I didn't get the account. My much-larger competitor did. They got it on price and are more than likely working their rear ends off on a case for very little money. At some point, they will also lose it on price. They were shortsighted to do it for this pricing because they ended up costing everybody money when they proposed the ridiculous rate they were willing to do it for. It's below the industry norm, and this client is underpaying. We were already the two finalists, and both of us had fair pricing on the table. Nobody needed to drop rates, and the decision could have been made based on who the client wanted to work with at a fair pricing level. The competition just made us both losers. I get no money on the deal but don't have to work; they get a little money but have to work too hard for it. Either way, we both lost.

If a current client or prospective client puts you in this kind of a position, I strongly suggest you check your ego, forget about winning, and get out while you can. If you have competitors willing to do too much work for too little money, let them.

If you do not have a value proposition other than your lower price, you are still going to win sometimes, just as my larger competitor did in the aforementioned scenario. But you are going to be working way too hard for the money. Price cutting to ridiculous points is something that people who are scared or weak do. Do not make that the basis of your company. Just because you might be able to cut prices farther than a bigger company to get business doesn't mean that someone else isn't going to be able to undercut you at some point and take that non-desirable, low-profit client right off your client list next year. Easy come, easy go when you get clients on price. It's a slippery slope; avoid it.

What you need is a *real* value proposition. One that is more value to a client than a few percentage points of price cutting from your vulture competitors. During your paid training at your current employer, look around and figure out what they are not giving clients that they should be. What is it they could be offering clients to make their product or service superior? When you know the answer, you know your differentiator.

CHAPTER 24

Money to the Client

The value proposition in the differentiator you create for clients *can* be about saving them money. It can't be about lower prices though. I know that sounds like I'm contradicting myself, but I'm not. The best sales presentations are ones that actually have the client paying *more* for a product or service than the competition is offering, but at the same time demonstrate to the clients how it is still going to financially benefit them. The service or product being offered is worth more money because it is going to either make them money or save them money in other areas.

Now we are talking about a win-win situation. Create that kind of value proposition and then go find the clients who will listen. That client, my friend, is the client you want on your books—they value you and your product and respect you. They didn't buy from you because you had the lowest price that you may or may not be able to maintain in the future.

In some products and services, it is easy to connect the dots between what you're selling and how it can translate into money for the client. For instance, if you are selling website ad space to businesses at a higher cost than your competitors, you should talk about the larger number of people who see the space you're selling versus what the client is currently using. You then connect that the additional exposure leads to additional clients for that company, which then leads to additional revenue—thus having your higher prices make complete sense. You don't need to spell it out quite like that to a client as it could come across as condescending, but you do need to make a clear connection to how *your* product or service is going to make or save *the client* money.

What if you have a product or service that is harder to connect those dots with? Think hard about it and find the dots to connect. You have a much greater likelihood of making the sale if the person buying sees your product as something that is going to make or save him money—rather than just something that makes his or his employees' lives easier, more joyful, or safe. Always tie it into the money! This is especially true if what you are selling isn't replacing a cost the client already had but is going to serve as a new line item on the budget. You better come up with a way to show the client the money. Business owners like to hear about their ROI (return on investment) on any purchases.

Example 1:

If you are selling group vacation packages to corporations to buy for their employees, you aren't selling how cheap the Rio de Janeiro package is and how much the employees will love it. You are selling a means to keep employees more productive at work and decrease turnover.

HERE IS YOUR VALUE PROPOSITION:

Happier employees are more productive employees—this will result in an increase to your top line of X in the next two years, Mr. Client. A 20 percent reduction in turnover will save you Y dollars in finding and training new employees. As you can see, my product's price is more of an investment than anything else as it will pay for itself Z times over in the first twenty-four months.

You aren't selling how fun it would be for employees to get these vacations for cheap; you are selling how it's a smart decision from a financial standpoint for the client.

Example 2:

If you are selling security and surveillance equipment to retail outlets, you aren't selling that you are going to keep the bad guys out. You are selling the money the client will be saving in the future.

HERE IS YOUR VALUE PROPOSITION:

By purchasing this equipment, Mr. Client, you are going to have a vast reduction in retail theft from your store. This will result in replacing X dollars less in stolen merchandise and will save you Y percentage on your insurance premiums next year.

You aren't selling how much safer the store is going to be; you are selling how it's a smart decision from a financial standpoint for the client.

Example 3:

If you are selling wrought iron fences and are pitching to a city parking lot. You aren't selling how strong the iron is and how it won't deteriorate. You are selling the money it's going to make the client.

HERE IS YOUR VALUE PROPOSITION:

By adding these fences to surround your lot, the lot will be more secure, and customers will recognize and appreciate that. They will be willing to pay an additional $1.50 a day to park. Based on the average number of cars you have each day, this will increase your revenue X the first year while the one-time cost of the fences is only Y.

You aren't selling how your fences are better than the competition; you are selling how it's a smart decision from a financial standpoint for the client.

Example 4:

You are selling dispatch services to taxi companies. You aren't selling the clarity in the system and how the dispatcher can more easily communicate to the drivers. You are selling the increased productivity by having the system.

HERE IS YOUR VALUE PROPOSITION:

By purchasing this more advanced system, your drivers will be able to respond to customer calls more expediently while fewer pickups will fall through the cracks. In the first year, this will result in a 15 percent increase in revenue to your company, which is roughly X dollars.

You aren't selling how advanced your new dispatching

technology is; you are selling how it's a smart decision from a financial standpoint for the client.

As you read those examples, you may have asked yourself, "How would I know the client's revenue and savings up front when doing my sales presentation?" Duh! You knew because you did your homework prior to going into the meeting and were readily prepared. If that kind of information is unavailable, you still need to find a way to make the point and show the return on investment in working with you. If you can get the information through diligence beforehand, your message will be much stronger.

It will be more difficult in some industries to come up with a way of tying your product's value to money for the customer. This is harder with commodity-type products, and also more difficult when selling luxury items. It is also tougher to do when the buyer isn't the business owner but instead an employee that has decision-making capabilities. Remember that those people still like making their boss (the business owner) happy, and I can tell you that making or saving money makes business owners ecstatic.

In your evaluation process, ask yourself if you have a way to do this for your future clients.

CHAPTER 25

Money to You

There are a lot of perks to being a business owner versus working for someone else besides money. There's the freedom to do things how you want them done and, most importantly, the ability to serve your clients' best interest without jumping through hoops and getting approval to get things done right.

Regardless of the other perks to being a business owner, the financial upside should still be a focal point.

Like Joe Pesci's character said in *Lethal Weapon*, "Money talks, BS walks." Sure, you may take a pay cut and you can make very little when starting out—that is okay. But you do not want to start a company that cannot survive and that doesn't have a financial upside to you.

In other words, if you are in a position where you are earning good money, don't leave it if you don't see yourself making money near that amount or more on your own in the short- to midrange future.

Look back at Chapter 10 ("How Much Does Your Company Make Off of You?"). Sit down and use that as your basis for what clients you feel like you are going to be able to get on your own and how profitable they will be in your business model. Be honest with yourself in determining how many clients you will get in years one, two, and three. Project a low, medium, and high-gross revenue then subtract the expenses you will have. Now compare those nine numbers (low, medium, and high for each of those three years) against what you are making right now. Looking only at the numbers in front of you, does this move make sense?

Oftentimes, we let our egos get the better of us and think of the glory of being a business owner as more important than the money we will use to pay our mortgage and put our kids through school with. If what you are making now is more than your high projections two and three years out, you need to look very, very closely at this decision and potentially consider aborting or delaying the idea.

Many books of this nature are "rah-rah!" books, encouraging you to start a business and motivate you to take the plunge. Here is a reality check: if the money isn't there when you do this part of the evaluation, come up with a plan B. Start over if you have to, and I don't care if it takes you another five years to come up with a plan B. I would rather see you being able to pay your bills than going broke trying to be a hero and feeding your ego.

As I stated before, business ownership *is* more than just the money. We have discussed having the freedom and control of your future. However, I have also mentioned the fact that there are employees in certain positions that have the ability to make big-time money. This part of the evaluation really is on you to weigh any financial downside versus the non-quantifiable benefits of freedom and control. Only you can decide what's important.

CHAPTER 26

Feel Out Your Clients

It would not only be unethical but also highly risky for you to discuss your potential new company with your current clients. I do *not* recommend that at all. What you should be doing is figuring out a way to gauge how important you are from the client's point of view. These are the kinds of people you will need to attract into working with you when you go out on your own, and they will be the best indicator of how talented you really are (in their eyes, which is all that matters).

Before you go on your own, you should subtly communicate with clients to see what they think of you. And when I say "before," I don't mean the day you are about to leave. I mean months prior. Find creative ways to ask them this without implying or mentioning a thing about you starting your own company.

I will give you examples of a couple questions and also show some good and bad replies.

ᕯᕯᕯ

Subtle question 1:

You: We are thinking about moving things around in the management of your account and I wanted to see what you thought of some potential team changes? There is nothing set in stone and it won't happen for a while, but we are talking about it, so I wanted to hear what you thought.

By asking this question, you allowed the client to share their thoughts. You didn't make your employer look bad, and it comes off as a totally legitimate question. It gives the client the sense of power in how this will be unfolding, therefore not angering the client.

RESPONSES TO QUESTION 1 FROM CLIENTS:

Client A: Well, they aren't taking you off our account, are they? If they move around the others, that is okay, but I definitely want you on this still.

Boom! That is a good answer—that's what you want to hear with this question.

Client B: It would really depend on what you mean by team change? I don't really want much change, but I guess I can live with whatever as long as the new person is good still.

Although not as good as client A's response, it still isn't terrible. It's okay since the client said, "As long as the new person is good *still*" at the end. By using the word "still," the client just called you "good" and is hopeful that the new person is as good as you. It's still complimentary.

Client C: *Well, I know that your company is great with a lot of great people, I'm sure the new team members will be excellent.*

This is the wrong answer. The client doesn't care if you leave; you didn't show anything to that person.

Subtle Question 2:

You: *Are you happy with the resources you get from other people in our office? Like my manager and support staff?*

The purpose of this question is to gauge how relevant services and other people at your company are to the client.

Responses to question 2 from clients:

Client A: *What people and resources?*

That is more than likely a good answer. Assuming the client is a happy client, this means that it is all *you* who's making him happy. If he is not a happy client, this response could mean that he isn't impressed with your company or you, and that he is only with you because he wants to avoid change or hasn't gotten around to it yet.

Client B: *Yes, they are good; I appreciate everything you guys do for us.*

This is a "middle of the road" response, with the only positive piece of it being the use of "you guys" in it—meaning you at least are appreciated as well as the company.

Client C: I am very happy. Just the other day, your manager called and explained to me the new program you are rolling out . . .

Any response like this that gives specific examples of experiences your clients have had with people translates to them feeling comfortable with people at that company besides you. This is the worst kind of response you can get . . . they aren't leaving to go to your new company when you leave.

(By the way, take note when management at your employer is regularly contacting your clients and capitalizing on relationships you built. This is management's way of preparing for retaining these clients if you were to leave the company. Nope, they aren't as dumb as you thought.)

◢◢◢

Hopefully you get the gist of this. I don't suggest you use these exact questions, but you can certainly use variations of them that make sense in your industry and your company. If your company has a non-compete agreement, you should still ask these types of questions to your clients. Not because you want to violate your non-compete and take these clients with you, but because it will give you an understanding of how good you are in these clients' eyes, which will help you gauge how appealing you will be to future clients.

CHAPTER 27

Don't Ask for Dieting Advice from a Fat Guy

Would you ever walk up to a fat person and ask him what the best way to lose weight is?

The answer is obvious—of course you wouldn't. In the same way, don't ask someone who has never taken the plunge into starting their own business or done anything entrepreneurial for advice on how you should.

This is especially true for the veteran, top salesperson at your current workplace. Asking that person is wrong for two reasons actually:

1. He doesn't know what it takes because he never did it.

2. He is drinking heavy company Kool-Aid and will tell you what a terrible idea it is to go on your own, and how you could never compete with organizations like the one you currently work at.

He has to say that and think that. If he doesn't, he will be admitting he either (1) isn't as smart or as bold as you or (2) should have done so as well.

Instead of asking the top veteran salesperson for advice on starting your own company, ask him for advice on sales techniques—that is why you are there in the first place (paid training).

Another person you want to avoid asking advice from is any of your family members or friends. That is unless they started their own company presently or in the past. Realize that everyone is not wired like you to be thinking this way, and most people are worried more about security and safety— societal Kool-Aid, if you will. The evaluation processes in this book, when performed honestly and thoroughly, should address any issues regarding security. Nobody else will have thought this through like you, so don't let the off-the-cuff comments from relatives deter you from something you have put a lot of time and effort into considering.

Your family and friends may very well have your best interest at heart with their advice, but what do they know if they never have done it? Also, the whole envy factor could come into play if you really do have a plan that works, so you may not get an honest opinion anyway.

You also don't want to go to your manager or boss for advice on this. You're not going to get an honest answer there regarding *anything* that could potentially have ill consequences on the company you currently work for—especially on this question.

I remember when I was in my second year at my first job. I qualified for the company sales conference in Hawaii, and it was considered a big honor to be invited on the trip. Around the same time, I tried out for some new reality TV show that was going to be on ESPN.

Lo and behold, I made the show! It was going to film for three weeks and involved travel all over the country. I went to get advice from my manager on whether or not I should do the show, as doing it meant that I would miss the Hawaii sales conference. I had the vacation time built up, so that wasn't an issue.

Well, my manager was pretty firm about telling me it's a bad idea and how it "will look" to upper management. I ended up not doing the show and going to the sales conference. I did this because of my loyalty to my company and the career path that I was committed to. It was probably the right decision to make, but I look back now at how that unfolded and realize things that I didn't realize then:

1. My manager didn't want me to go, not because I would look bad; it was because *he* would look bad to upper management for having a sales rep he hired skip the conference for a TV show.

2. My main motivation was loyalty to my company and not sending a red flag to upper management . . . two years later, the entire upper-management team had turned over. I can guarantee that the new people would not have cared if a sales rep did or didn't go to a conference two years prior while under the previous management team, all of whom got fired.

Now, if you go ask your manager his opinion on whether or not you would succeed with your own company, do you really think you're going to get an unbiased, honest answer? I couldn't even get an honest answer about why I should or shouldn't go on a reality TV show.

If I could go back in time, I probably would have made the same decision regarding that TV show . . . but I would have made it for myself. I wouldn't ask my manager for his advice on it, knowing that he would have personal interest in the decision.

The same goes for starting your own company. Starting a business is interesting and unique, just like being asked to be on a reality show. If you ask someone who has never been asked to be on a reality show or started their own business their opinion if you should pursue it, they will have the innate response of "bad idea" nine times out of ten.

As you evaluate starting your own business, be very choosy in deciding whose opinions matter to you. Find somebody who you can trust with no ulterior motives and who has accomplished launching their own company. Talk to people who have been successful with their businesses, ask them questions on what has worked and what hasn't worked, then take the information they give you and figure out what is relevant to you. Don't be so narrow-minded as to consider only the information that you want to hear and ignore the bad parts. This is a big decision, and you have to be honest with yourself about it and broaden your mind.

You asked those people advice for a reason—because they

have the experience of doing this. It's in your best interest to get something out of the information they give you. If they have an opinion about your model that they disagree with or don't like, explain yourself more thoroughly and ask them why. If they are in a different industry, they may not understand everything you know about your industry. Make them understand it then get their opinion again. If they still don't like something, take that into heavy consideration as you make your next move.

Other business owners are the ones to ask for diet advice. Your co-workers, your family, and your friends are the fat guys.

CHAPTER **28**

The Complexities of Being a Business Owner

Let's say you are good at what you do currently, you are successful, and you have determined you are able to get new clients and retain them. You also need to determine if you have it in you to run a business yourself. There is more to it than just getting the clients to come.

There will be a learning curve, but the most important thing is your ability to get new business and keep it. I found that as long as the clients and the money are coming in, you can figure out everything else as it happens. A lot of the problems that arise are good problems to have. For instance, very early on I found out the hard way that the IRS tax reporting rules change dramatically when your business grows over $250,000 annual gross. I also found out at the end of the year from my CPA that my documentation and reporting requirements are immensely more involved. I didn't sit there and wish my company would have made less that year.

I figured out my taxes. Had I consulted with my CPA earlier in the year and told him how much I was going to make, I wouldn't have had this problem. However, I really didn't know I was going to make that. I had to get a bunch of old bank statements and credit card invoices sent over to me. It cost me some money, but mostly time. In the end though, I figured it out and realized it wasn't that big of a deal. You will face these same challenges—good challenges—with success.

There are also going be other issues that you will not encounter until your business gets bigger and you get more clients. There are things like the infrastructure and setup of your phone lines, Internet, and network. There are services from phone companies that will make your life easier or you will have to adapt to. There are better fiscal ways to run things in terms of supplies and deliverables once your volume is greater and the need to start making purchases for your company in bulk exists. All of these are good problems to have to face.

What you don't want to do is bog yourself down with items like these when they are irrelevant. Think of them on the surface, but don't spend too much time on them until you actually need them.

I look back at some old internal documents I was using during my first year in business. I was tracking revenue and had a number of advanced spreadsheets outlining anything from client-by-client profitability, to office supply costs, to a comparison of office space options down to the nickel. All are good things for me to be aware of, but ultimately, what I found is that if the clients and the money are coming in, all of that other stuff will take care of itself. My worst option in that situation is better than the best option if I don't have revenue coming in.

Corporate company Kool-Aid will often overwhelm a person into thinking that all of these things are unmanageable and can discourage him to take the leap. They really are manageable.

Take advantage of the fact that you are no longer in Corporate America as an employee, you no longer have to attend weekly sales meetings, turn in detailed expense reports, or have regular manager review sessions. You can now focus the majority of your time on ways to get new clients and service them better.

Now don't get me wrong, you will have to be able to run a business—even if the business is just you at first. You will no longer have an IT guy to run to when your Internet is down. You are no longer going to have a $5,000 color LaserJet printer to print out your proposals right down the hall. You are going to have to deal with these things yourself.

I remember when I first hired an assistant in my second year in business. I gave her a salaried, full-time position. I made an employee handbook outlining company benefits, vacation time, dress code policy, and even our policy on things like sexual harassment and steps in reporting sick leave. In essence, I spent a lot of time doing things that didn't have anything to do with me getting new clients or being able to service existing ones better. But once she started, I realized I didn't really have enough work for her to do anyway. I could have done most of it myself. I didn't need to hire an assistant at that time after all; in so doing, I put a lot of time and effort into non-client-oriented services.

It was a mistake, and I was not taking advantage of one of the very reasons I became a business owner—to have more time to focus on my clients and not get caught up in corporate mumbo jumbo with meaningless reporting and meetings. My advice to you: Don't make this same mistake.

Incorporating your business is a very easy process. Hire a lawyer for $500 or just do it online yourself. I'm telling you—IT'S NO BIG DEAL to incorporate. You will figure it out rather easily, and to demonstrate my point, I'm not going to waste space in this book discussing that further.

If you are completely disorganized, like some salespeople tend to be, you do need to consider the types of things you will need to be capable of to run a business. This will vary from industry to industry, and there will be licensing, bonding, and insurance requirements that you may need to obtain. Let me assure you: all this is manageable, so do not feel overwhelmed. You are walking into unchartered territory, but believe me when I say that I found that territory to be pretty "charterable." Getting the services of a lawyer and a CPA would be my suggestion if you want to feel more comfortable.

Remember, focus on selling and bringing in new clients—everything else will take care of itself. It's okay to make some mistakes in the beginning. You will learn it as it happens.

Section 5
Making the Move and Some Start-Up Advice

You double checked to make sure you have extra ammunition.

You reviewed your itinerary and know exactly where the enemy is at.

You made sure your canteen is full.

You came up with a plan that you are confident will put you in a position to win.

It's now time to go to war.

CHAPTER **29**

When You've Stopped Learning, Get Out

If you regularly find yourself running in place, with no real advancement of knowledge, it's time to consider making the move. You need to be sure you are ready though. You should use all of the previous lessons from these chapters in making that decision, and always, *always,* BE HONEST WITH YOURSELF.

For a long time before I made the decision to leave, I had felt like I was just there, not accomplishing anything. I was looking around at other people in the office, thinking to myself, "Are you kidding me?" or "Is this person serious?" I was in weekly sales meetings, feeling like it was a complete waste of time. I was giving reports to managers and felt like it was just a hoop to jump through so the manager and I can feel as if we are filling up our day with work.

I had stopped learning. I knew I had learned enough.

When this starts happening to you, it's time to go, and it's time to go soon. Hopefully you have already analyzed and developed the skill set necessary to be on your own; if you haven't, you still need to get the heck out of there.

Throughout this book, I hope I have made my point that during this process, you are supposed to be a good and productive employee. This book does not encourage unethical behavior; it's supposed to encourage you to give the company you work for your best while taking the knowledge to be your best when you leave. If you get to that mundane state where you start acting as if everything around you is phony or a waste of time, you will inevitably become viewed as a "bad employee" sooner or later, which breeds animosity from your former peers when you move on your own. Naturally, this will more likely earn your brand-new company a built-in enemy (your former employer) on day one. You don't need that. No new company needs that.

If you leave on a high note, animosity is less likely to occur. Instead, your managers and co-workers are more likely to have a "good for him" and "wish you luck" attitude. There will always be envious people who'll hope you'll fail regardless of how amicably you leave your employer—but you are certainly better off if you don't give them a reason to act that way toward you. Leaving on a high note prevents this. Being a cynical, non-company man in your last few months will make it difficult for anyone there to be happy for you.

You're starting your own company because you are good at what you do and you created the path to do it. You didn't get there by being a horse-crap employee; don't let this be your colleagues' last impression of you.

When you've stopped learning and growing, you won't be able to "fake it" as an interested, good employee for very long. Recognize this early and time up the leave promptly. If you are still walking into the office every day with a bounce in your step and learning new things, it may not be time to leave yet.

CHAPTER 30

Speak the Language, but Don't BS

One thing I've learned since starting my own company, from competing against other much-larger firms, is that sales representatives from the bigger, older firms are able to get away with some things in the way they present and sell that I can't. And, may I mention, these are things that I don't really *want* to get away with anyway, but only the sharpest consumers are going to be able to see through it. Most others are going to allow such because of the credibility this person has as a representative for the large, fifty-plus-year-old, billion-dollar organization. If I said those same things (which I wouldn't say regardless of where I worked), I'd be pushed for further information or a clearer explanation from the prospective client.

Let me give you an example of what I'm talking about. In the business world, a lot of buzzwords or clichés make their rounds. People will use such words or phrases to sound smart or sound like they know what they are talking about, but what are they really saying?

Nothing.

Case in point:

I know in the environment we are currently working in, it's important that we put the fires out proactively and adapt to the ever-changing issues presented in this arena. It can appear to be quite a daunting task at times, but you should rest assured that our team of professionals is prepared for the actionable items necessary to deliver the desired results of our clients.

I laughed as I typed that. If I ever said anything like that to a client, I would wait for him to kick me out of the office. If the client didn't, I'd do it myself and then fire me. It's a bunch of industry buzzword BS that really doesn't mean anything. The sharp consumer isn't going to allow a statement like that to fly without some follow-up probing. However, many consumers, when hearing it from a person with an established company's logo on his business card, will nod their heads and act as if the cure for cancer was just revealed.

As a small company, you can't get away with the same BS that a salesperson for a larger organization can get away with. The credibility is not there; people don't know who you are. You need to back up what you are saying with clear and concise language. If you don't, and instead just use industry buzzwords, you can bet that the sales rep from the bigger company is saying the same BS. If you were the decision maker, would you buy the same pile of BS from the billion-dollar company or from the brand-new little guy? Make the decision easier for him and don't sell the same BS.

Your vocabulary needs to be good and your industry knowledge needs to be great. However, just make sure that when you speak, you are actually saying something.

CHAPTER 31

Inflate Your Company, Not Your Head

Unless you have something so desirable that people are going to be buying from you no matter what, I highly recommend *not* naming your company after you. I also recommend not putting *President, Owner, Founder*, or *CEO* on your business card or in the signature line of your e-mail.

I pounded the pavement when I first started on my own, and I was really happy about a few things I did in positioning myself. I named my company "Northwest Comprehensive, Inc." Notice that I didn't name it "John Cerasani Insurance" or anything that had to do with my last name.

Furthermore, the directional usage in the title makes it seem like my company is more established, and people often associate such word usage with other companies that use similar titles—psychologically implying to the client that this company has been around for a while. In fact, I've had some prospective clients tell me that they've worked with my firm twenty years prior (which they didn't, as it didn't exist yet). The name I chose implies established and big . . . something that can make a prospective client more comfortable.

The other key ingredient was that I always positioned myself as a seasoned sales rep or consultant to clients. I never lied if asked what the ownership structure of my company was, but I didn't run around touting myself as the owner or president either. I'm simply a good, polished salesperson representing a company that the client has never heard of. Doing this gives credibility to the company since in the client's eyes, it has such an established professional working for it (if I do say so myself).

Adversely, going out there and positioning myself as "John Cerasani of Cerasani Unlimited, LLC," does not establish credibility and, if anything, only serves as a detriment. I would be swimming upstream. For what I sell, there are people besides who I am presenting to that need to put their stamp of approval on the matter. If I made all the sense in the world and the person I presented to liked me and recognized my value, I can still get shot down when he goes to his peers and superiors for the final approval and says he is recommending, "John Cerasani, the president of Cerasani Enterprises" for this project. It screams "SMALL TIME." That wouldn't be the case if he recommended "John Cerasani, the senior consultant from Northwest Comprehensive, Inc."

Position yourself as a sales consultant working *superbly* for an *outstanding* company. Be excited about your product or service, and professionally explain the reasons a client should work with you. There is no need to mention you own the company—it can only do harm. Remember, you are trying to get a new client, not a new girlfriend.

To the sharpest and most savvy decision maker, names and titles do not matter. But why risk having it get in the way? Perception is everything, and if you are selling business to business, there will often be people who are aware of or have an influence over which firms their company is going to be working with that you will never meet. The bottom line is, don't give them an excuse not to work with you because of the name you chose for your company.

CHAPTER **32**

This Isn't the Adult Film Industry

Bigger is *not* better.

However, "Bigger is better" is an issue that inevitably comes up for almost any new, small company choosing to compete against larger, established competitors. For that, you need to have a reason that *you believe* and can articulate to the client. If you don't believe it, you need to ask what you are doing in the first place.

Have a value proposition that you can give to your clients that your larger competitors cannot.

I have made it clear to my clients—and they believe me because it's true—that there are advantages to working with my company instead of a large, publicly traded, ten-thousand-plus-employee organization. Below are some of them:

- *A greater percentage of revenue associated with an account is used toward servicing that account, thus making the client experience that much better.*

In other words, we use the money we make to service our accounts the best way possible. Our bigger competitors have to use portions of that revenue for other expenses that have nothing to do with servicing the client, such as the salaries of multiple layers of management, dividends to shareholders, irrelevant resources, and various corporate departments that don't exist at smaller companies.

- *The person presenting and selling to the client is also going to stay involved in the client's account.* This allows for smoother integration and assures that clients get what they were promised during the sales process. Bigger organizations often have salespeople that either leave the equation after the sale is made or, at the very least, shift their priorities to finding the next sale even if on the surface they are still technically involved.

- *If a client has a unique need, our organization can adjust and be flexible.* This is much harder to do at a larger organization, especially if it involves any change in revenue or profitability on an account. A smaller organization can make such a decision quickly and act on it without multiple layers of corporate bureaucracy.

I can go on and on with various ways a smaller company can be better than its bigger competitors; some will be true for your business and some will not. You need to be ready to answer that question, and you need to have an answer that you truly believe in. If you don't believe it or are wishy-washy about it, then the answer is not good enough. Find one that is.

Some clients will counter anything you say on this matter. For me, it's almost funny when this happens. It often becomes clear that no matter what I say, it's not going to matter to this particular client. The reason, 99 times out of 100, is that the person I am dealing with has to make a recommendation to the *real* decision maker, whereas he doesn't want to be questioned on why he chose a little, new company. Hey, if he chooses the billion-dollar company and it screws up, it wasn't his fault, right? He chose the big guy, they are the best! But if he recommends the little, unknown company, then his head might be on the chopping block if there is a screw-up. This is a tough situation to be in as the real decision-maker has delegated the duty to someone else, and you aren't going to get in front of the main guy.

I have rebuttals on hand for this type of scenario, and you should too.

If and when I am told that my competitor has more experience or knowledge than I do, I prepare two questions. Depending on the audience, I need to be careful not to offend or come across as arrogant, but still get my point across. In this kind of situation, you are dealing with someone who is either scared or who just doesn't get it. If he tells you another company is better than your company, probe him to make sure there is a tangible reason (their competitive advantage over you) . . . *if* there is one.

- "Who at the hundred-year-old company that would be servicing your account has hundred years of experience?"

- "If I got hired there and they then gave me a business card with their logo on it, would they then put a microchip into my brain to give me more knowledge than I have today? If not, why would you put more credibility on their sales rep's advice just for working there than on advice from me?"

These two questions will hopefully surface the problem and change the way the conversation goes. If they don't, I don't have anything to lose anyway as this person is too scared to go against status quo, and a new company is not ever going to be status quo.

CHAPTER **33**

Control What You Can Control

I had the opportunity to play football one year for a gentleman named Randy Walker. He took over for Gary Barnett before my senior year, after Barnett jumped ship on Northwestern. Walker, who died suddenly in 2006, had some great one-liners that I was privileged to hear. One of my favorites was, "Control what you can control."

Control what you can control:

- Don't worry about what we should have done last week differently to win the game; worry about who we are playing this week.

  » Don't worry that you lost in a finalist presentation to someone you should have beaten yesterday; worry about the prospect call you have today.

- Don't worry that our starting quarterback is hurt; worry about getting the backup ready to play.

» Don't worry about the prospect not having projector capabilities for your PowerPoint; worry about making the best-looking binders this prospect has ever seen.

▪ Don't worry about not being able to pass the ball in the snowstorm; worry about making sure our running game is strong.

» Don't worry about the fact that this client isn't going to care that you offer online billing; worry about finding something else that will matter to him.

As you get started, you are going to be faced with many challenges from prospective clients. You are going to be questioned on credibility and on whether or not you will still be in business in the future. You will have to go head-on into such situations and ready yourself for some tough questions from prospects. You will not be able to hide from the fact that you have only been in business for two months or two years. You will not be able to hide from the fact that you don't have a huge staff or huge client list.

What you *do* need to worry about are the things you can control. You don't need to have been in business for decades to demonstrate responsiveness and great customer service. You showed up to the meeting on time, and you were punctual with your follow-up promises. You represent yourself as a professional and demonstrate strong industry knowledge. You come across as impressive because of your passion for what you are offering.

Clients like that. That won't be enough for all of them, but for others, it will be just what the doctor ordered. It will be a breath of fresh air versus what they are used to. You have shown them that superior customer service standards still do exist and that you will bring it to them.

Before you know it, you'll already have a couple of references as existing clients. The prospect on the fence between you or your bigger competitor is now pushed over the top. He not only sees how service oriented you are but also now gets references to call that back that up further. *Boom!* Now you are snowballing in the right direction.

CHAPTER 34

Pulling the Trigger

Timing up your move is usually a tough decision for most people. Sometimes it's an easy one though. It really depends on how obvious things are to you in evaluating your job and the industry you are in. Hopefully, as you read this book, some things jumped out that make the picture a little clearer for you.

For me, once I had the epiphany, things became so ridiculously easy for me. People told me how brave I was and how much courage it took to leave my comfy, white-collar job and go out on my own. I didn't see it as a risk at all. I knew what I was jumping into, from evaluating my industry and myself. I was confident that going on my own was going to result in a raise in income in the first twelve months, and I was right.

I thank people and tell them "Yeah, it was a tough decision," when they tell me about what an admirable risk-taker I was for doing it. The reality, however, was that I'd have to have been a moron not to do it. The epiphany I had and the series of evaluations that followed it made the path simple.

Now, in fairness, I also benefitted from the culture of where I was employed at the time. There were some functions of my former job that made it pretty easy to walk away from. For instance, when warm leads or opportunities were given to the management, they weren't being passed along to the top performers. Or if they were, they weren't being passed to this top performer. I remember feeling like it was almost a socialist or communist sales environment, where the guys making something out of nothing and hitting their numbers (i.e., *me*) were not given the "layups." Instead, some of the guys struggling were. Almost as if we all needed to be around the same figure in our year-end sales numbers and things should be evened out.

I didn't really realize this was happening until my epiphany. I guess you can say it was part of it. I can't criticize my old employer though; I was twenty-seven years old at that time, and that was just my perception. They were obviously doing something right over there as they are a billion-dollar organization. I just didn't want to be a piece of that puzzle anymore.

Also, I felt that I didn't need to stick around. I didn't dislike my job, I didn't dislike the people I worked for. But I didn't see the path for great financial gain and recognition I thought I was capable of within that culture. That made the decision to leave that much easier for me. I knew that I didn't need the job as I was confident I could do it on my own.

However, even with that understanding, I asked for a raise before I left. A pretty big one, but not an unrealistic amount either. I didn't get it. Had I gotten it, I would have stayed there. Not getting that raise may have been the best thing that ever happened to me career-wise, but I'd like to think that it would have just delayed the inevitable, and I would have still gone on my own sometime after that. The epiphany was there; it was just a matter of me acting on it. The timing will never be perfect; there will never be a right or wrong. The only wrong is not doing it if the evaluation process has demonstrated that you are capable of succeeding with your business idea.

If you feel underpaid or underappreciated, whether it is in a sales job or service job, your decision to leave that job will be that much easier. However, remember that that feeling of under-appreciation needs to be legitimate in your self-evaluation process. The decision on timing up your move comes *after* your thorough evaluation.

You might be in a much harder position than I was if your job is great and you do see a path there. Remember this: head-hunters and recruiters for the best jobs are calling people with great current jobs—they aren't calling people that are unemployed or in bad spots. Or if they are, the employer that's hiring isn't hoping for those candidates.

When you start your own company, that job has the potential to be the best job you can ever imagine—the perks, the income, the benefits, and the recognition. Unfortunately, no headhunter will be calling you to tell you about it. If you concluded in your evaluation that you are ready and able, suck it up and do it. There is nothing to wait for. If you didn't have good opportunities available to you working for someone else, you probably wouldn't have concluded you can pull off success on your own anyway. You're in a good spot with options, now pull the trigger.

The easiest position you can be in (for this piece, at least) is that you got laid off (unwarrantedly) or are between jobs. Make the move then; you have nothing to lose with no current job at risk. Remember, even if you are not completely confident that you can be a success, you can learn some things as you go. This is not the ideal path, as your paid training may not be complete yet, but if you are far enough along where you are "close," it may not make any sense to use your time and effort in trying to find another job that you are probably going to leave in a few months to go on your own. It may give you the additional confidence, but stop and really think about whether or not it is imperative.

Remember that nobody is going to do this for you. There isn't going to be a post on your Facebook wall telling you it's time to quit your job. You're not going to get an anonymous text message telling you it's time. It's more than likely going to involve some anxiety and risk; but your evaluation process should give you confidence. At some point, you are going to have to just do it.

The other side of this, to be master of the obvious, is that you need to be able to pay your personal expenses with no income when you first start out. We all have different fixed expenses for our lives, and the "ramp-up period" for when your business actually starts making money is going to depend on a number of factors.

That said, make sure you have enough money to survive. You don't want to be in a situation where you *need* a sale to pay your mortgage—this could send you on the slippery slope of price-cutting early on and position your company as such in the marketplace. You don't want to be known as that, and you don't want clients that seek that. Make sure you are okay with your personal finances when you get going; you will have enough to worry about with other aspects of your business to add that to the mix.

One may argue with my last paragraph, stating that it's good to be hungry and need the sale. I disagree. If you are working for someone else and are in a commission-based sales position, I can buy into that argument. Business owners don't need that kind of motivation; you already have the passion to succeed.

CHAPTER 35

Create Your Luck

As you have read through these chapters, I am hoping that some realizations took place—perhaps even an epiphany of your own. You may have purchased this book because you are not happy at your place of employment, and this outlined the path you should take into going into business for yourself. Or you may have purchased this book because you were already committed to going into business on your own, but now you have discovered some areas you need to address prior to doing so. Or maybe this book reaffirmed what you already knew and suspected about being your own boss.

Whatever your reason for reading this book, please be honest with yourself as you think through what's next for you. Oftentimes, we let emotions get in the way of reality. We want something to be true so badly in our head that we make it true even if it's false. That optimistic mind-set is great in many of life's capacities, but *not* when making this decision. Remember that before you run and quit your job: you still need to feed your family and save for retirement. Make sure your evaluation of yourself and your industry, as outlined in this book, chapter by chapter, shows you that your business being a success is true. There can be risk—nothing wrong with that—but limit the risk by having a plan from the lessons of each of these chapters.

Remember the dramatic upside potential in owning a business versus remaining an employee when evaluating if the risk you have ahead of you is worth it or not. When I was in my early twenties, I bought four residential properties to rent out with minimal down payments. When I was an employee, I was hoping to break even on my cash flow each month as I had to balance the rent versus the mortgage payment and other expenses. My financial gain from being a business owner has since allowed me to pay off the mortgages, resulting in very positive cash flow every single month.

I also came across an opportunity while a business owner that allowed me to invest as a silent owner in a very risky restaurant venture. Had I been an employee still, there would have been way too much risk to take on that endeavor. Now that I had the extra capital, I found it to be a risk I could easily tolerate if the restaurant went south. The investment worked out, and I get a nice check every month from what has turned out be an ultra-popular destination in downtown Chicago.

Being a business owner provided me with the income to open up the doors to other opportunities. As an employee, these doors would have remained locked. Keep this in mind as you weigh the risk versus the reward in starting your own company. The reward has huge upside potential, and you should see the risk as somewhat limited after closely following the steps that this book has laid out.

When I took the leap, I never looked back. After being a successful business owner for a few years, I started to evaluate why I was successful and wondered if the stars were just aligned for me. Was I just lucky?

I have often used the word "fortunate" when describing why my business was successful. Maybe it was luck or fortune that got me here, but I can tell you that it was luck that I created for myself. I didn't realize it at the time, but the entire evaluation that I showed you throughout this book is what I was doing for a solid two years while working for someone else. This preparation brought me the "luck" that led to my company's success.

My company is still up and running and stronger than ever; if you get to the point where your company starts offering employee benefits insurance, you should consider my company. Visit www.NWC-USA.com to contact me (*that's called a shameless solicitation, by the way*).

You now have this spelled out for you. You have a road map that will guide you. You are in a better spot than I was. If you are honest and real about who you are and what you are capable of, you will ultimately make the right decision. I encourage you to visit me online for further discussion at www.PAID-TRAINING.com.

Throughout the book I often compared your small start-up company to the biggest and best in your industry. Keep in mind that there will be other small and medium companies you will be competing with as well. My stance has always been that if I found a way to beat the most successful competitors (the big guys), I'd be able to beat the little guys too. Take the same approach if you take this leap and aim high.

The world needs entrepreneurs as well as good employees; it doesn't need bad employees. Whatever direction you take, create your own luck. There is no need for me to wish it upon you.

CPSIA information can be obtained at www.ICGtesting.com
Printed in the USA
LVOW07*2305301014

411344LV00002B/8/P